Monet

1840-1926

Grange BOOKS

Page 4:
Auguste Renoir,
Portrait of Claude Monet, 1875
oil on canvas, 85 x 60.5 cm
Musée d'Orsay, Paris

Designed by:
Baseline Co Ltd
19-25 Nguyen Hue
Bitexco Building, Floor 11
District 1, Ho Chi Minh City
Vietnam

ISBN 1-84013-749-5

© 2004, Sirrocco, London, UK
© 2004, Confidential Concepts, worldwide, USA

Published in 2004 by Grange Books
an imprint of Grange Books Plc
The Grange Kingsnorth Industrial Estate
Hoo, nr Rochester, Kent ME3 9ND
www.grangebooks.co.uk

Printed in China by Everbest Printing Co Ltd

Foreword

It was Claude Monet's *Impression: Sunrise* painted in 1873, which caused disapproving critics to contemptuously apply the name (Impressionist) to the whole movement with which he was associated. Here is a magnificent collection of the great master's works. There are many full-colour plates of his earlier works, such as the famous *Lady in the Garden Sainte-Adresse* (1867) and *The Pond at Montgeron* (1876-1877) in both of which the artist's extraordinary ability to capture atmosphere and light are shown in starkly contrasting scenes. Examples of several of the series of paintings of the same subject which Monet was fond of producing – *Haystacks*, *Rouen Cathedral*, the *London* series – are included here, as are his numerous depictions of his favourite resorts, Sainte-Adresse and Etretat on the Alabaster Coast of Normandy.

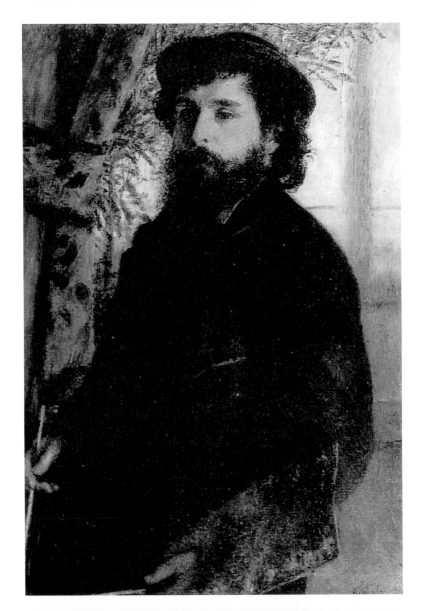

Biography

1840: November 14, Claude Oscar Monet is born in Paris.

1845: The Monet family moves to Le Havre.

1858: Makes the acquaintance of Boudin, who introduces him to plein-air painting.

1859: Goes to Paris. Meets Troyon. Frequents the Académie Suisse, where he meets Pissarro.

1860: Draws at the Académie Suisse. Paints landscapes at Champigny-sur-Marne. In the autumn, is called up for military service.

1861: Serves with the army in Algeria.

1862: Discharged for health reasons. In the summer, works at Sainte-Adresse together with Boudin and Jongkind. In November, returns to Paris. Attends the studio of Gleyre. Meets Renoir, Sisley and Bazille.

1863: Works at Chailly-en-Bière near Fontainebleau. At the end of the year Monet, Renoir, Sisley and Bazille leave the studio of Gleyre.

1864: Works at Honfleur with Bazille, Boudin and Jongkind. In Paris, meets Gustave Courbet.

1865: Exhibits two seascapes in the Salon. Spends the summer at Chailly together with Bazille. In the autumn, works at Trouville with Courbet, Daubigny and Whistler.

1866: Paints views of Paris. Exhibits *Woman in a Green Dress* (Camille) in the Salon. Meets Edouard Manet. At Ville d'Avray, paints *Women in the Garden*; in Le Havre, *The Jetty at Le Havre*; then works at Sainte-Adresse and Honfleur.

1867: Experiences financial hardship. Lives with his parents at Sainte-Adresse. In the autumn, returns to Paris.

1868: Works at Etretat and Fécamp.

1869: Together with Renoir, works at Bougival, where he paints *La Grenouillère*. Moves to Etretat, then to Le Havre.

1870: In September, goes to London.

1871: Stays in London. Daubigny introduces him to Durand-Ruel. Meets Pissarro. Travels to Holland. Reveals an interest in Japanese prints. Returns to France visiting Belgium on his way. In December, stays at Argenteuil.

1872: Together with Boudin, visits Courbet imprisoned for his participation in the Commune. Works at Le Havre, where he paints *Impression. Sunrise*. After his second trip to Holland settles at Argenteuil (until 1878).

1873: Works at Argenteuil in a studio boat, painting the banks of the Seine.

1874: Shows nine works at the exhibition later to be called the First Impressionist Exhibition held at Nadar's (April 15-May 15, 35 Boulevard des Capucines). Meets Caillebotte.

1875: Continues to work at Argenteuil. Difficult financial situation.

1876: In April, takes part in the Second Impressionist Exhibition, at the Durand-Ruel Gallery (11 Rue Le Peletier), showing eighteen works. Begins the *Gare Saint-Lazare* series, which he finishes the next year.

1877: In April, participants in the Third Impressionist Exhibition (6 Rue Le Peletier), displaying thirty paintings. Visits Montgeron. In the winter, returns to Paris.

1878: Settles at Vétheuil.

1879: At the Fourth Impressionist Exhibition (April 10-May 11, 28 Avenue de l'Opera) shows twenty-nine paintings. Works at Vétheuil and Lavacourt.

1880: His one-man show at the premises of the newspaper La Vie Moderne. Works at Vétheuil.

1881: Works at Vétheuil, Fécamp and, in December, at Poissy.

Claude Monet

1882:	In March, at the Seventh Impressionist Exhibition (251 Rue Saint-Honoré) shows thirty-five paintings. Works at Pourville, Dieppe and Poissy.
1883:	In March, his one-man show at the Durand-Ruel Gallery. In May, stays at Giverny. Works in the environs of Vernon, in Le Havre, and at Etretat. In December, makes a short trip to the Mediterranean with Renoir. Visits Cézanne at l'Estaque.
1884:	From January 17 to March 14, works at Bordighera. In April, stays at Menton; in August, at Etretat; in the autumn, at Governy.
1885:	Takes part in the International Exhibition at the Georges Petit Gallery. From October to December, works at Etretat.
1886:	A brief trip to Holland. Refuses to take part in the Eighth (last) Impressionist Exhibition. Contributes to the International Exhibition at the Georges Petit Gallery. A show of Monet's paintings in New York. In September, works at Belle-Ile, where he meets Geffroy.
1887:	Shows two paintings at the Exhibition of the Royal Society of British Artists in London.
1888:	From January to April, lives at Antibes. In July, visits London. In September, returns to Etretat.
1889:	In July, exhibition of works by Monet and Rodin (145 pieces) in the Georges Petit Gallery.
1890:	Begins the *Haystacks* and *Poplars* series. Moves to Giverny.
1891:	Continues his work on the *Haystacks* and *Poplars* series. The *Haystacks* series enjoys a success at the exhibition in the Durand-Ruel Gallery. In December, visits London.
1892:	Exhibits his *Poplars* series. Begins the Rouen Cathedral series.
1893:	Continues his work on the Rouen Cathedral series.
1894:	Cézanne visits Giverny.
1895:	In January, travels to Norway. Shows his Cathedrals series in the Durand-Ruel Gallery (May 10-31).
1896:	In February and March, works at Pourville.
1897:	From January to March, stays at Pourville.
1898:	In June, takes part in the exhibition at the Georges Petit Gallery.
1899:	Begins the *Water-Lilies*. In the autumn, goes to London, where he paints views of the Thames.
1900:	In February, visits London again. In April, works at Giverny. Spends the summer at Vétheuil.
1901:	In February and April, stays in London.
1902:	Spends February and March in Brittany.
1903:	Works on views of the Thames in London.
1904:	Paints his garden at Giverny. Shows his views of the Thames at the exhibition in the Durand-Ruel Gallery (May 9-June 14). In October, goes to Madrid to see works by Velázquez.
1906:	Works on the *Water-Lilies* series.
1908:	From September to December, stays in Venice.
1909:	In the autumn, returns to Venice, where he paints a series of views.
1912:	Shows his Venetian series at the exhibition in the Bernhein-Jeune Gallery (May 28-June 8).
1916:	Begins work on the decorative panels the *Water-Lilies*.
1921:	A retrospective exhibition in the Durand-Ruel Gallery (January 21-February 2). In September, a short trip to Brittany.
1922:	Suffers from eye disease.
1923:	Works on the decorative panels the *Water-Lilies*.
1926:	December 5, dies at Giverny.

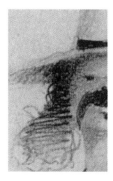

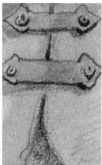

N umerous portraits of Monet have survived — self-portraits, the works of his friends (Manet and Renoir among others), photographs by Carjat and Nadar — all of them reproducing his features at various stages in his life.

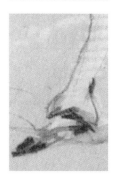

The Painter with a Pointed Hat

drawing

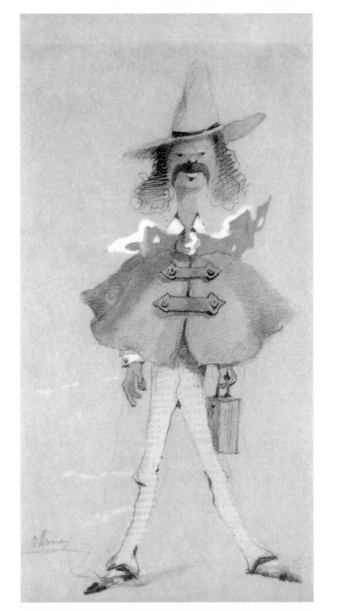

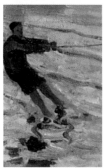

Many literary descriptions of Monet's physical appearance have come down to us as well, particularly after he had become well-known and much in demand by art critics and journalists. In 1919, when Monet was living almost as a recluse at Giverny, not far from Vernon-sur-Seine, he had a visit from Fernand Léger, who saw him as:

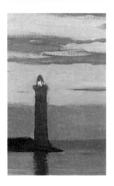

The Towing of a Boat in Honfleur

1864
oil on canvas, 55.5 x 82 cm
Memorial Art Gallery
of the University of Rochester, New York

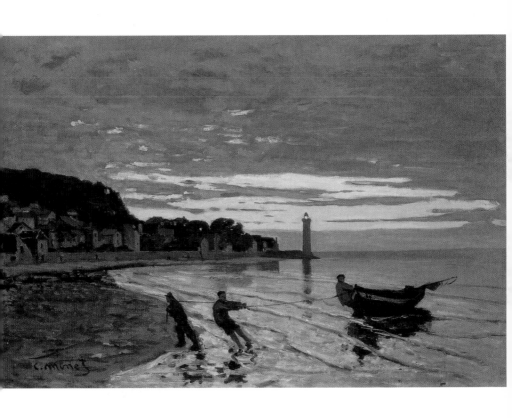

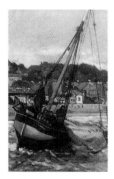

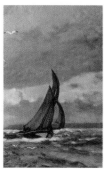

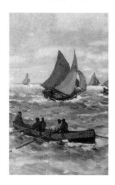

"a shortish gentleman in a panama hat and elegant light-grey suit of English cut… He had a large white beard, a pink face and little eyes that were bright and cheerful but with perhaps a slight hint of mistrust…"

Mouth of the Seine River in Honfleur

1865
oil on canvas, 90 x 150 cm
Norton Simon Museum, Pasadena, California

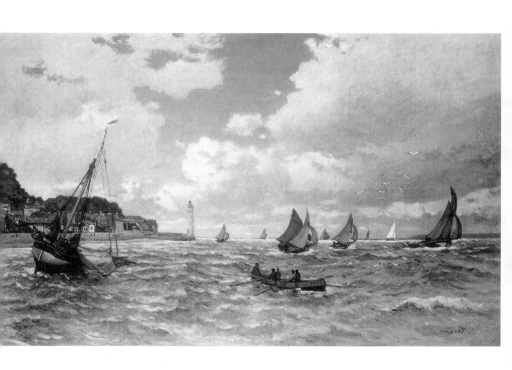

13

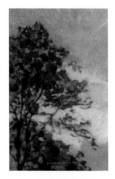

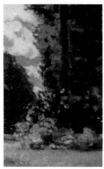

Both the visual and the literary portraits of Monet depict him as an unstable, restless figure. Monet's abrupt changes of mood, his constant dissatisfaction with himself, his spontaneous decisions, stormy emotions and cold meticulousness, his consciousness of himself as a personality moulded by the preoccupations of his age, set against his extreme individualism —

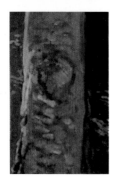

The Pavé de Chailley
in the Forest of Fontainebleau

1865
oil on canvas, 97 x 130 cm
Ordrupgaarsamlingen, Charlottenlund-Copenhagen

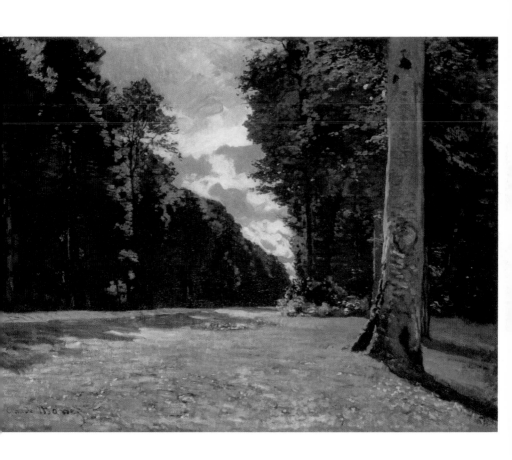

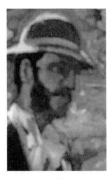

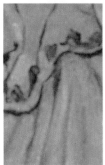

taken together these features elucidate much in Monet's creative processes and attitudes towards his own work. Claude-Oscar Monet was born in Paris on November 14th, 1840, but all his impressions as a child and adolescent were linked with Le Havre, the town where his family moved in about 1845.

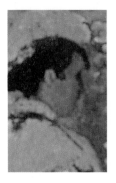

The Promenade

1865
sketch for the painting *Luncheon on the Grass*
oil on canvas, 93.5 x 69.5 cm
National Gallery of Art, Washington

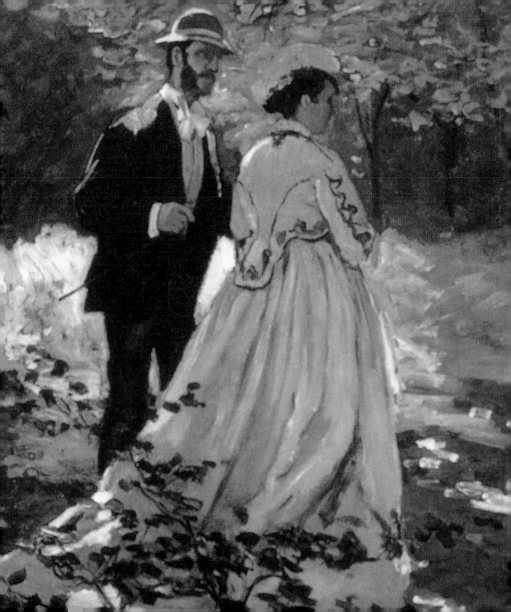

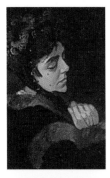

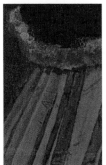

The surroundings in which the boy grew up were not conducive to artistic studies: Monet's father ran a grocery business and turned a deaf ear to his son's desire to become an artist. Le Havre boasted no museum collections of significance, no exhibitions, no school of art.

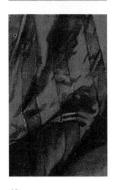

Woman in a Green Dress
(Camille)

————

1866
oil on canvas, 231 x 151 cm
Kunsthalle, Bremen

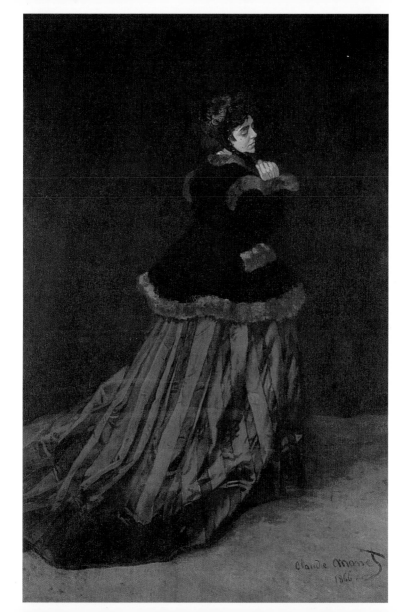

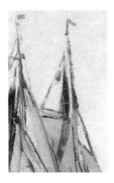

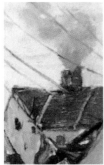

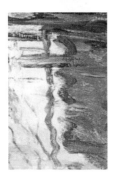

The gifted boy had to content himself with the advice of his aunt, who painted merely for personal pleasure, and the directions of his school-teacher. The most powerful impression on the young Monet in Normandy was made by his acquaintance with the artist Eugène Boudin.

Boats in Honfleur Harbour

1866
oil on canvas, 49 x 65 cm
Private collection

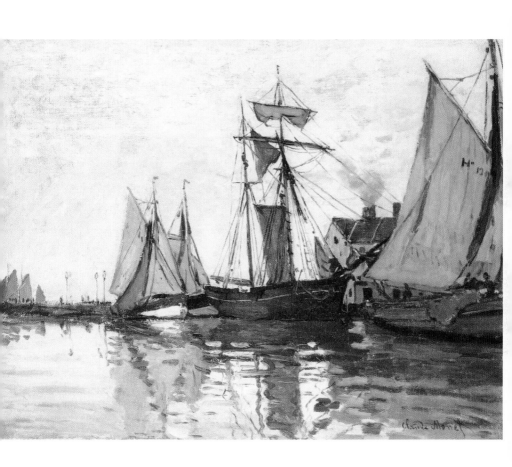

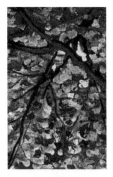

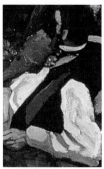

It was Boudin who discouraged Monet from spending his time on the caricatures that brought him his initial success as an artist, and urged him to turn to landscape painting. Boudin recommended that Monet observe the sea and the sky and study people, animals, buildings and trees in the light, in the air.

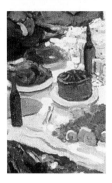

Luncheon on the Grass

1866
oil on canvas, 130 x 181 cm
The Pushkin Museum of Fine Arts, Moscow

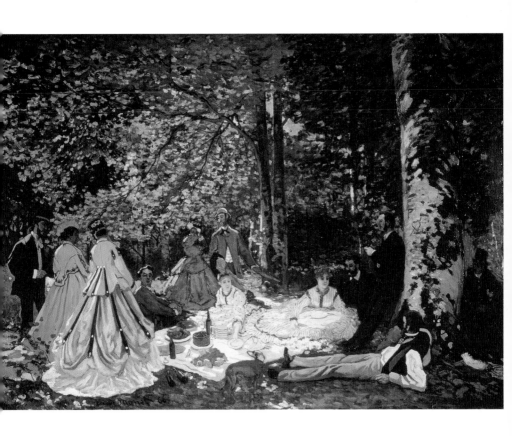

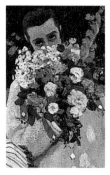

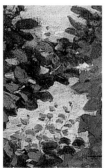

He said: "Everything that is painted directly on the spot has a strength, a power, a sureness of touch that one doesn't find again in the studio". These words could serve as an epigraph to Monet's work.

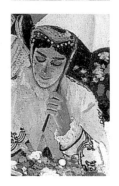

Ladies in the Garden

1866
oil on canvas, 256 x 208 cm
Musée d'Orsay, Paris

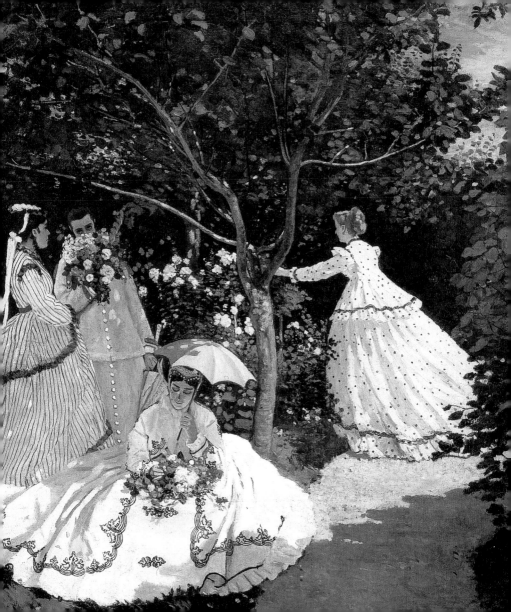

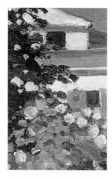

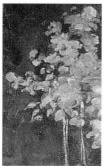

Monet's further development took place in Paris, and then again in Normandy, but this time in the company of artists. His formation was in many ways identical to that of other painters of his generation, and yet at the same time his development as an artist had profoundly distinctive individual features.

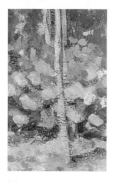

Garden in Blossom

about 1866
oil on canvas, 65 x 54 cm
Musée d'Orsay, Paris

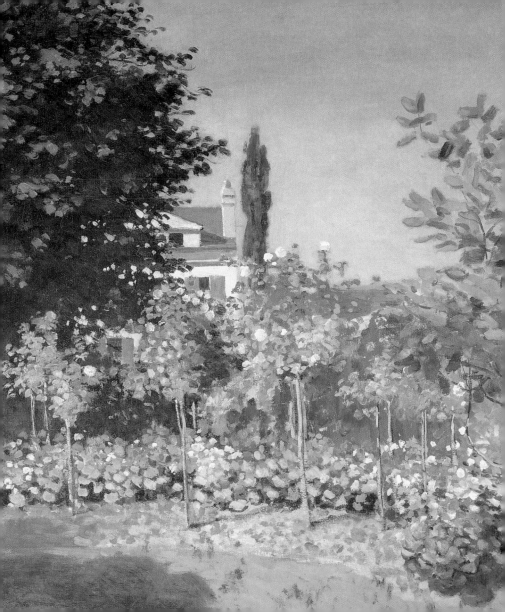

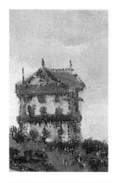

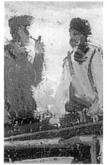

Monet preferred current exhibitions and meetings with contemporary artists to visiting museums. A study of his letters provides convincing evidence that contact with the Old Masters excited him far less than the life around him and the beauties of Nature.

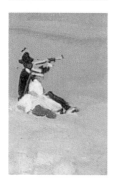

Beach at Argenteuil

1867
oil on canvas

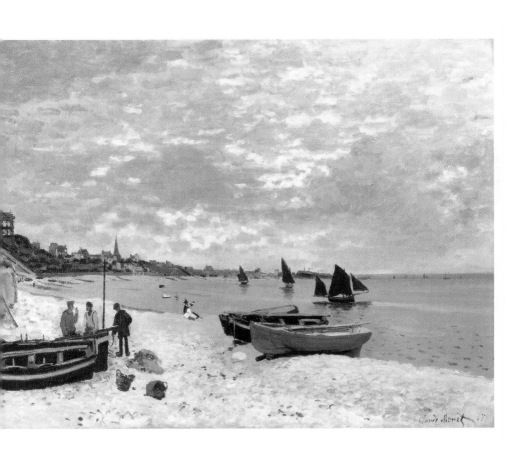

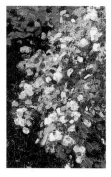

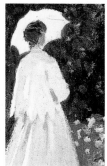

What then did particularly strike Monet during his first trip to Paris in 1859? An exhaustive reply is found in his letters to Boudin from Paris after his visit to the Salon. The young provincial passes indifferently by the historical and

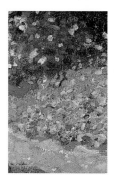

Lady in the Garden Sainte-Adresse
(Jeanne Marguerite Lecadre in the Garden)

1867, oil on canvas, 80 x 99 cm
The Hermitage, Saint Petersburg

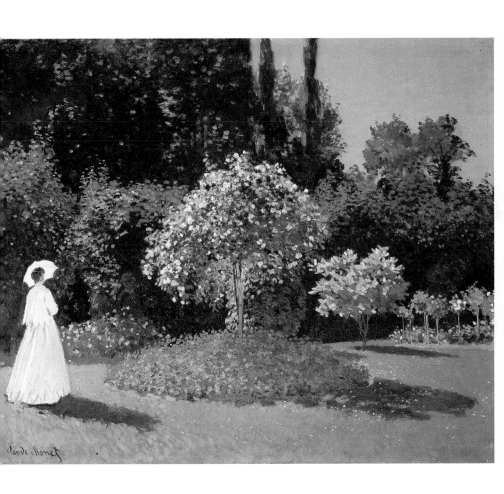

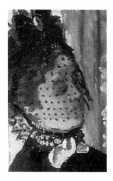

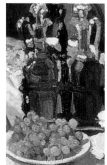

religious paintings of Boulanger, Gérôme, Baudry and Gigoux; the battle-scenes depicting the Crimean campaign do not attract him at all; even Delacroix, represented by such works as *The Ascent to Calvary, St. Sebastian, Ovid, The Abduction of Rebecca* and other similar subject paintings, seems to him unworthy of interest.

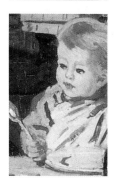

The Lunch

———————

1868
oil on canvas, 230 x 150 cm
Städelsches Kunstinstitut und Städtische Galerie
Frankfurt

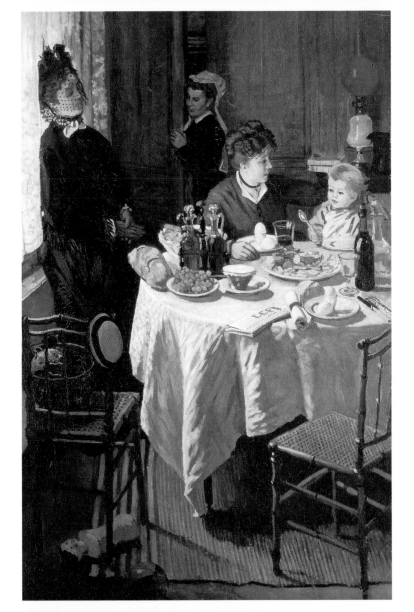

33

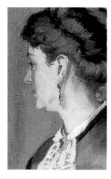

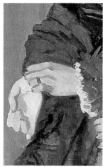

Corot on the other hand is "nice", Theodore Rousseau is "very good", Daubigny is "truly beautiful", and Troyon is "superb". Monet called on Troyon, an animal and landscape painter whose advice Boudin had earlier found valuable.

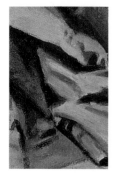

Portrait of Madame Gaudibert

1868
oil on canvas, 216 x 138 cm
Musée d'Orsay, Paris

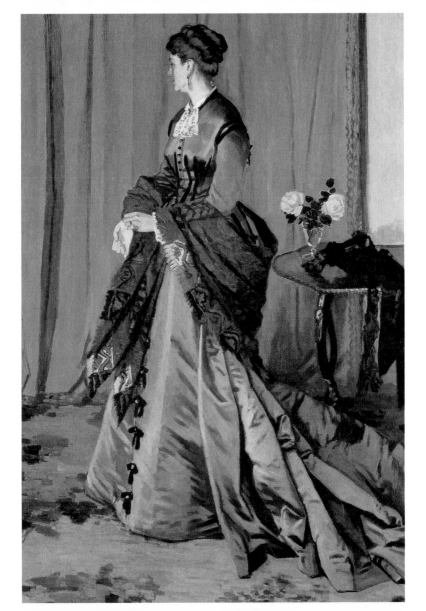

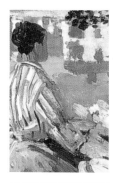

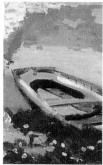

Troyon made recommendations which Monet relayed in his letters to Boudin — he should learn to draw figures, make copies in the Louvre, and should enter a reputable studio, for instance that of Thomas Couture. Monet thus immediately identified the figures who would provide his artistic guidelines.

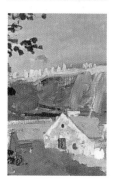

At the Water's Edge, Bennecourt

1868
oil on canvas, 81 x 100 cm
The Art Institute of Chicago

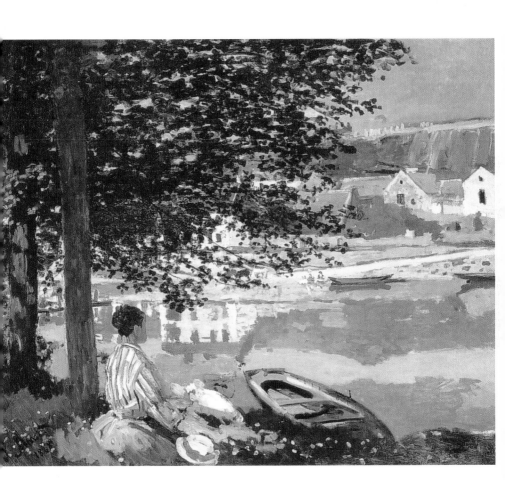

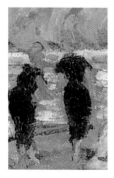

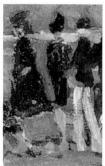

These were the landscapists of the Barbizon school, who had pointed French landscape painting towards its own native countryside; Millet and Courbet, who had turned to depicting the work and way of life of simple people; and, finally, Boudin and Jongkind, who had brought to landscape the freshness and immediacy lacking in works of the older generation of Barbizon painters.

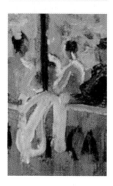

La Grenouillère

———————

1869
oil on canvas, 75 x 100 cm
The Metropolitan Museum of Art, New York

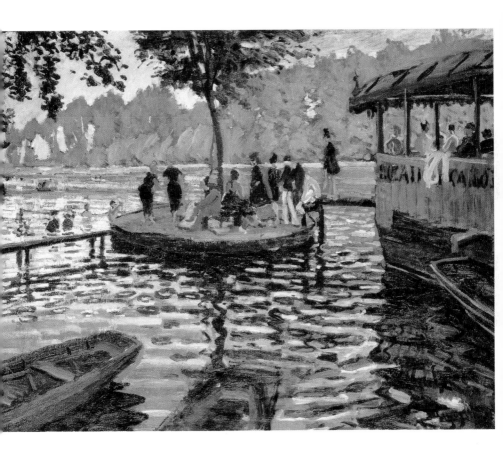

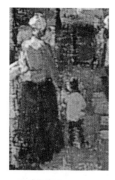

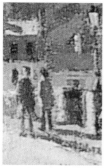

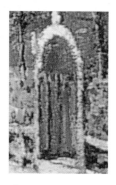

Monet was to paint alongside several of these masters — Boudin, Jongkind, Courbet (and Whistler, too) — and by watching them at work he would receive much practical instruction. Although Monet did not regard with great favour his immediate teacher Charles Gleyre, whose studio he joined in 1862, his stay there was by no means wasted, for he acquired valuable professional skills during this time.

The Bougival Bridge

———————————

1870
oil on canvas, 63.5 x 91.5 cm
The Currier Gallery of Art, Manchester
New Hampshire

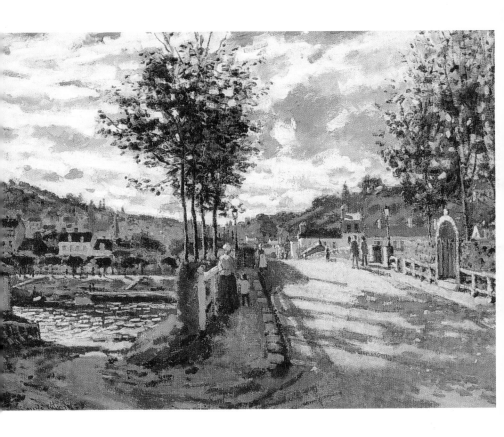

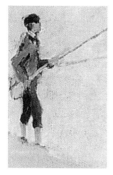

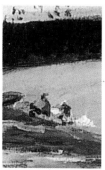

Moreover Gleyre, although an advocate of the academic system of teaching, nonetheless allowed his pupils a certain amount of freedom and did not attempt to dampen any enthusiasm for landscape painting. Most important to Monet in Gleyre's studio, however, were his incipient friendships with Bazille, Renoir and Sisley.

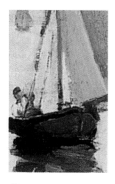

At the Entry of Trouville Harbour
────────────────────────────────
1870
oil on canvas, 54 x 66 cm
Szeépmuvészeti Mùseum, Budapest

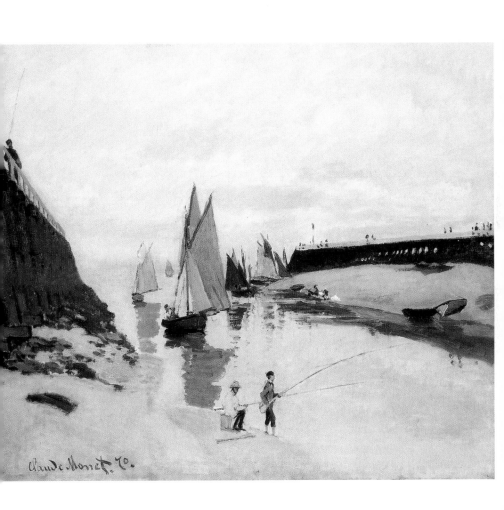

Claude Monet 70.

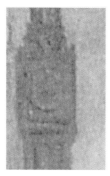

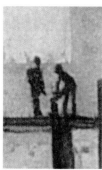

We know that he had already become acquainted with Pissarro, and thus it can be said that from the earliest stage of his career Fate brought Monet together with those who were to be his colleagues and allies for many years to come.

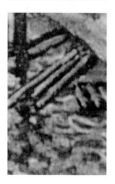

The Thames River
and the Houses of Parliament

1871
oil on canvas, 47 x 73 cm
National Gallery, London

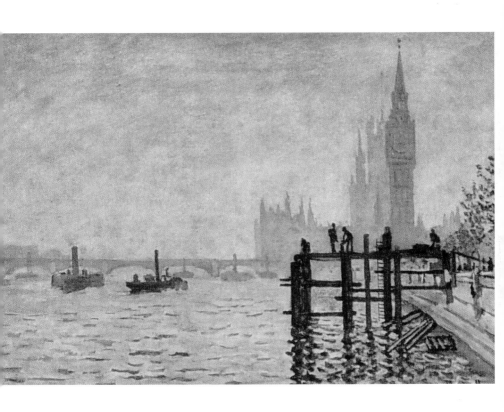

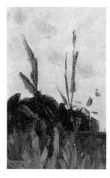

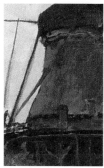

Manet and Monet knew one another's work long before they were introduced, and although at first very guarded in his attitude to Monet's artistic experimentation, the Batignolle group's leader soon became interested in him and began to follow the development of his work very attentively.

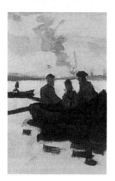

Mill in Zaandaam
_____

1871
oil on canvas, 48 x 73.5 cm
Ny Carlsberg Glyptotek, Copenhagen

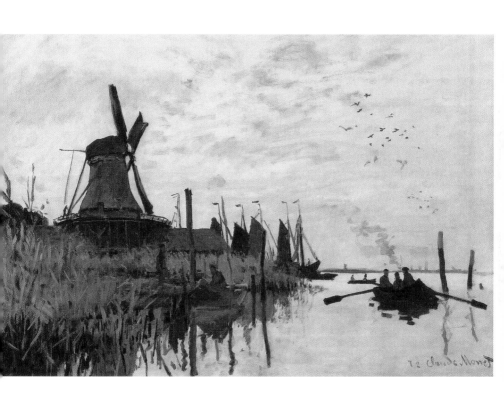

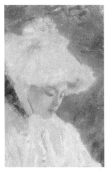

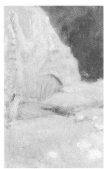

As far as Monet was concerned, he did not so much imitate Manet as imbibe the older artist's spirit of questing, gaining the impetus to release the powers latent within him. Monet's development was also influenced by his active contacts with Bazille, Renoir, Sisley and Pissarro.

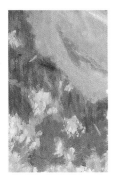

Woman Reading

—————————

1872
oil on canvas, 50 x 65 cm
Walters Art Gallery, Baltimore, Maryland

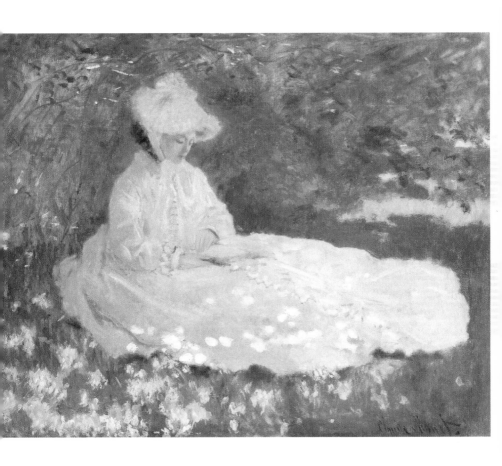

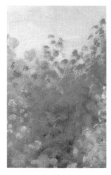

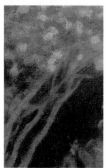

Discussions, arguments and, most important-ly, working together, served to sharpen the individual skills of each and facilitated the development of certain general principles. During the 1860s Monet had not yet determined his personal subject matter, but he had no wish to turn to historical, literary or exotic subjects.

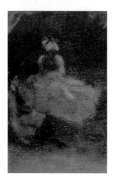

Lilacs in Dull Weather

1872-1873
oil on canvas, 50 x 65.5 cm
Musée d'Orsay, Paris

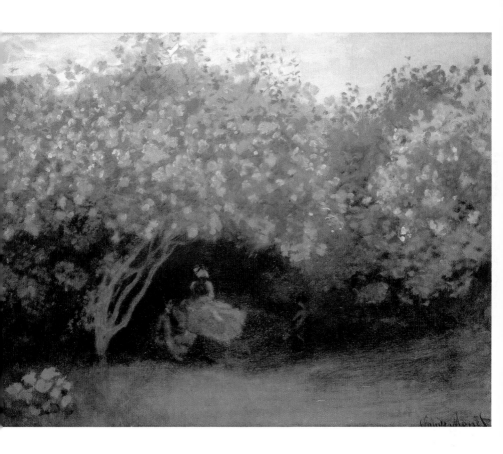

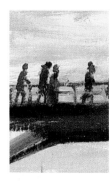

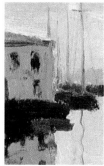

He made it his priority to serve the truth and to keep pace with the times, and only experienced a slight uncertainty in deciding whether the landscape or scenes with figures should be the genre central to his work. Like most artists of his generation, Monet evinced no interest in tackling acute social problems.

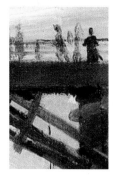

The Wooden Bridge
_____

1872
oil on canvas
Rau-Stiftung für die Dritte Welt, Zurich

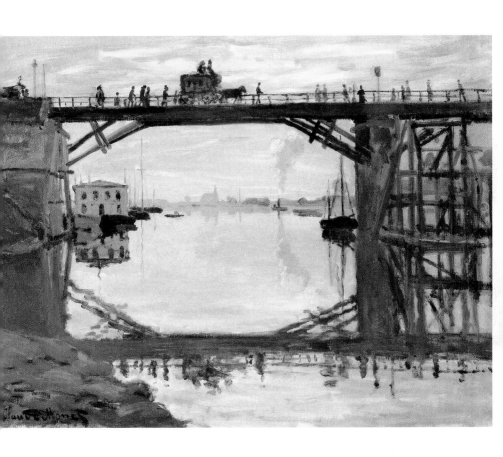

53

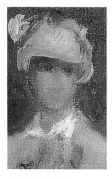

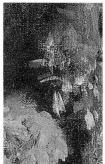

By the time Monet's generation began appearing on the artistic scene, the hopes inspired by the 1848 revolution had been shattered. Monet and his friends lived in the apparently unshakeable Second Empire headed by Napoleon III and supported by a bourgeoisie thirsting for wealth and luxury.

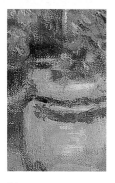

Camille Monet at the Window

_____

1873
oil on canvas, 60 x 49.5 cm
Virginia Museum of Fine Arts
Richmond, Virginia

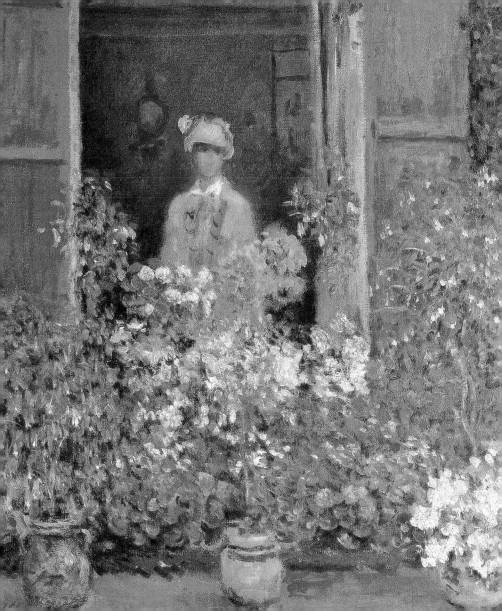

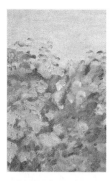

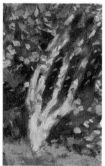

Progressive-minded artists longed merely to dissociate themselves, at least spiritually and morally, from the Empire. Thus Monet's genre paintings, which played a notable role in the first stage of his career, did not, unlike those of Honoré Daumier or Gustave Courbet, touch upon any vital problems in the life of society.

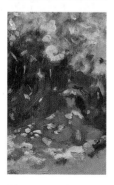

Lilacs in the Sun

1873
oil on canvas, 50 x 65 cm
The Pushkin Museum of Fine Arts
Moscow

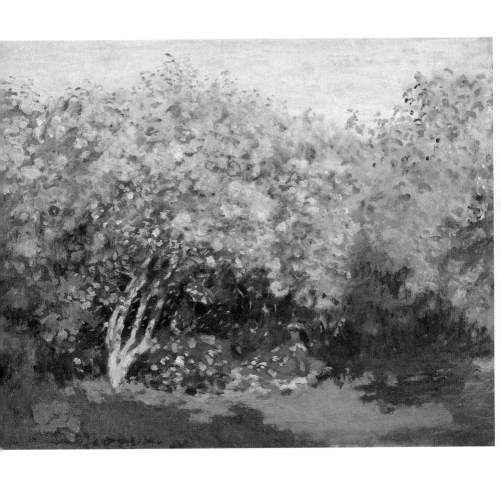

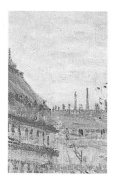

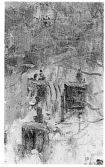

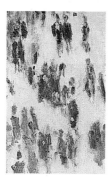

His figure painting was invariably confined to the representation of his intimate circle of friends and relations. Indeed, he portrayed Camille in a green striped dress and fur trimmed jacket — *Woman in a Green Dress* (1866, Kunsthalle, Bremen); Camille again with her son Jean at their morning meal —

The Boulevard des Capucines

1873
oil on canvas, 80 x 60 cm
William Rockhill Nelson Gallery and
Atkins Museum of Fine Arts, Kansas City, Missouri

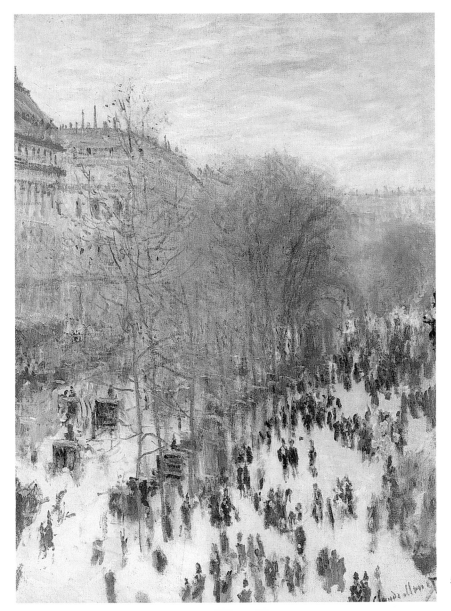

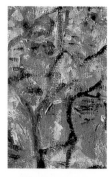

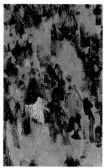

The Luncheon (1868, Städelsches Kunst-Institut, Frankfurt on Main); and the artist Bazille's sisters in the garden at Ville-d'Avray — *Ladies in the Garden* (1866, Musée d'Orsay, Paris). Two of Monet's canvases from the 1860s in Russian museums are similar in character — *Luncheon on the Grass* (1866, Pushkin Museum of Fine Arts, Moscow) and *Lady in the Garden* (1867, Hermitage, St. Petersburg).

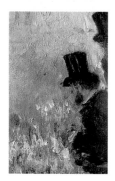

The Boulevard des Capucines

1873
oil on canvas, 61 x 80 cm
The Pushkin Museum of Fine Arts
Moscow

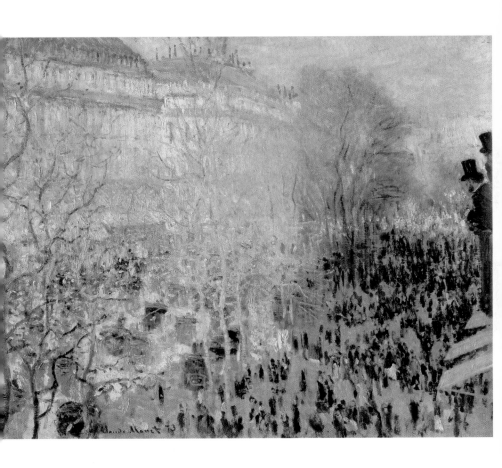

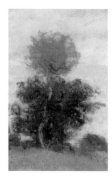

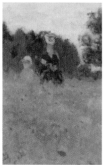

The first shows a group of friends having a picnic, among them Camille and the artists Frederic Bazille and Albert Lambron. The second depicts Monet's cousin, Jeanne-Marguerite Lecadre, in the garden at Sainte-Adresse. These paintings might seem to imply that the essence of Monet's talent lies in praise of the intimate and the everyday, and in the ability to recognize their beauty and poetry.

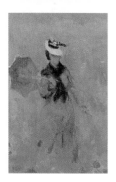

Poppies at Argenteuil

1873
oil on canvas, 50 x 65 cm
Musée d'Orsay, Paris

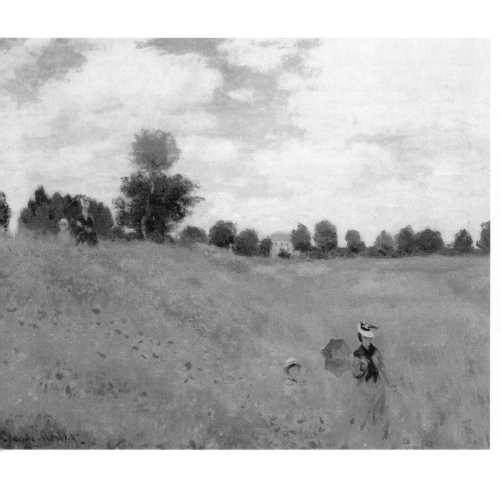

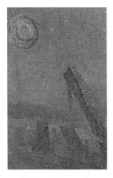

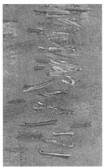

But Monet conveys these feelings with even greater depth, subtlety and variety when he turns to landscape. It can be seen from his figure compositions that he is not attracted by man's inner world or the complexity of human relations. He tends to accentuate the interaction between the figure and the surrounding natural world:

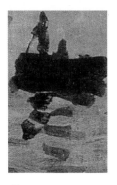

Impression. Sunrise

1873
oil on canvas, 48 x 63 cm
Musée Marmottan, Paris

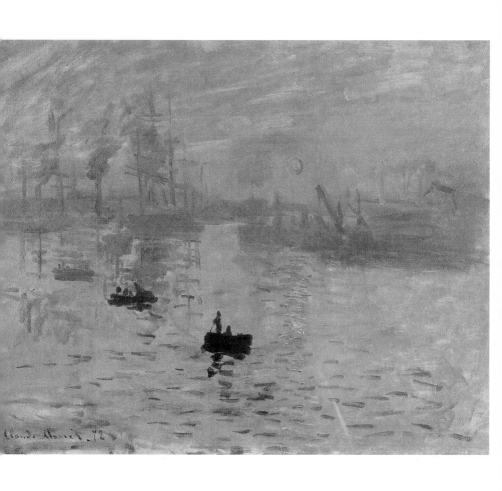

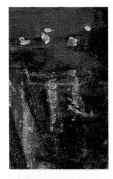

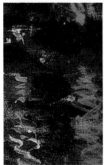

where the scene is set in the open air, the emphasis on the play of patches of light on clothing, or even the clothing itself, as in the *Portrait of Madame Gaudibert* (1868, Musée d'Orsay, Paris), rather than on a person's face. Clearly, by the early 1870s, Monet had fully recognized this feature of his talent, and figure compositions became less frequent in his work as all his powers were devoted to landscape.

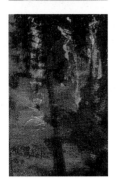

The Havre Harbour during the Night

1873
oil on canvas
private collection

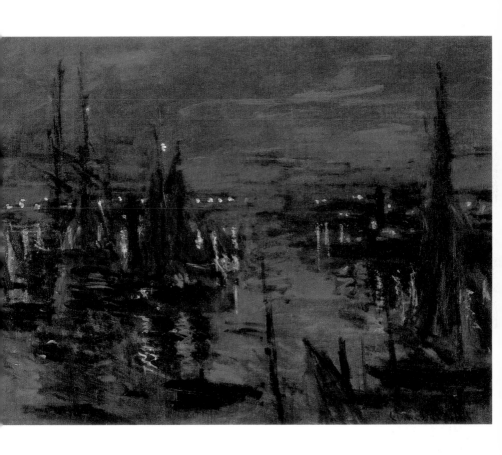

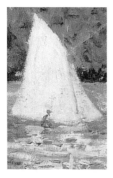

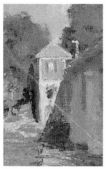

Nonetheless these early attempts at figure painting would benefit Monet in the future, for people appear in most of his landscapes — in fields, on roads, in gardens and in boats. True, man is by that stage not the main, nor even a secondary subject in a picture, but simply one of the indispensable elements of the changing world, without which its harmony would be disrupted.

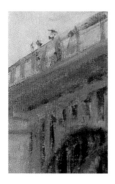

The Road Bridge. Argenteuil

1874
oil on canvas, 60 x 80 cm
National Gallery of Art
Washington (DC)

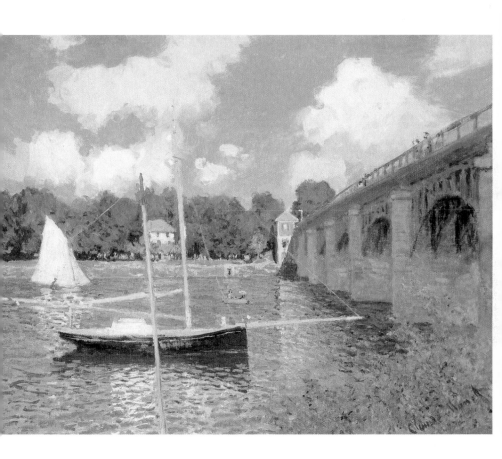

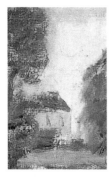

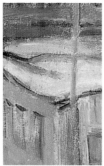

Monet almost seems to be reverting to the conception of Man and Nature reflected in Poussin's heroic landscapes; but in the great classicist's works Man and Nature were equally subject to the laws of higher Reason, whereas in Monet's they are equally subject to natural laws.

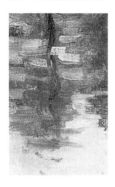

The Studio Boat

1874
oil on canvas, 50 x 64 cm
Rijksmuseum Kröller-Müller, Otterlo

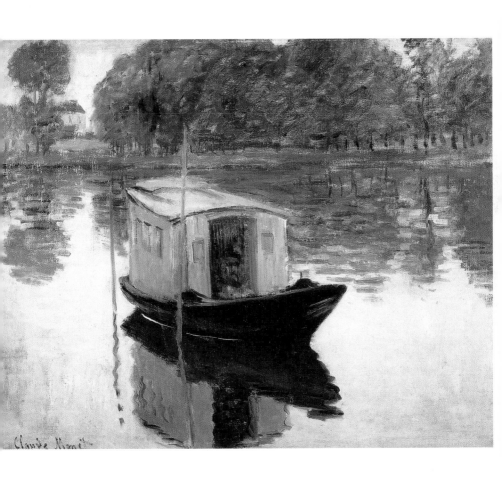

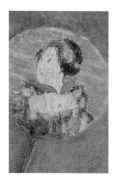

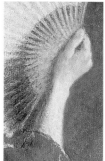

Another feature of Monet's landscapes in the 1860s and 1870s is that they are often more human than his figure paintings. This tendency can be explained not only by the fact that he was painting facets of Nature that were close and familiar to Man, but also by his perception of Nature through the eyes, as it were, of the ordinary man, revealing the world of his feelings.

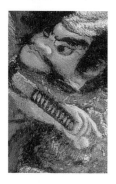

La Japonaise

1875
oil on canvas, 231.5 x 142 cm
Museum of Fine Arts, Boston

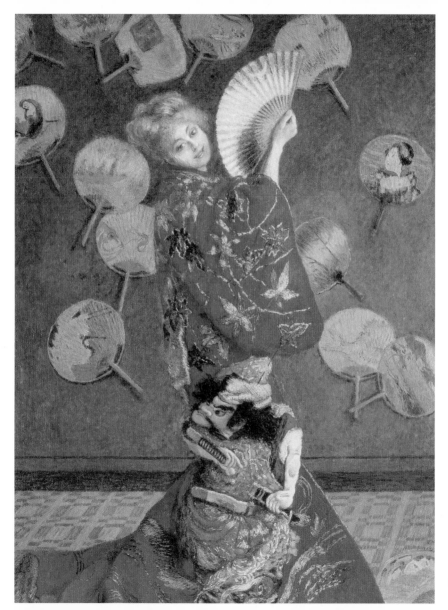

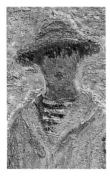

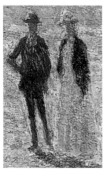

Each one of Monet's landscapes is a revelation, a miracle of painting; but surely everyone, so long as he is not totally blind to the beauty of his environment, experiences at least once in his life that astounding sensation when in a sudden moment of illumination, the familiar world he is accustomed to is transfigured.

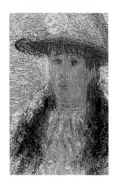

Landscape with Figures, Giverny

oil on canvas
private collection, USA

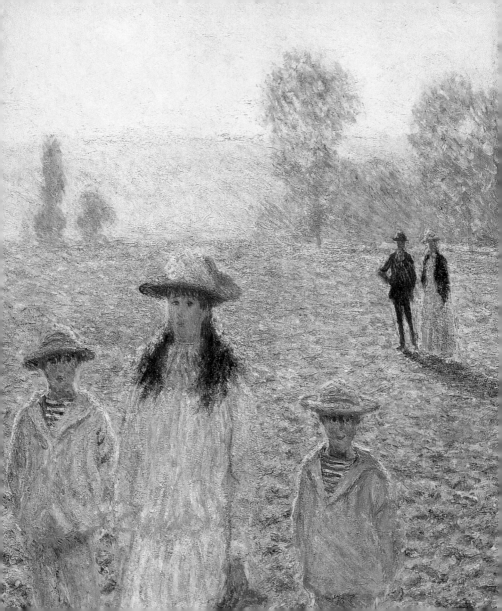

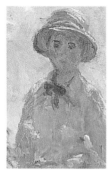

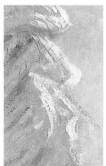

So little is actually needed for this to occur —
a ray of sunshine, a gust of wind, a sunset haze;
and Monet, as a genuinely creative artist,
experienced such sensations constantly. The
subject matter of Monet's early landscapes is
typical of his work as a whole.

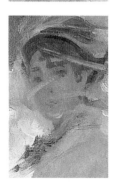

The Promenade
The Woman with a Parasol

oil on canvas, 100 x 81 cm
National Gallery of Art, Washington (DC)

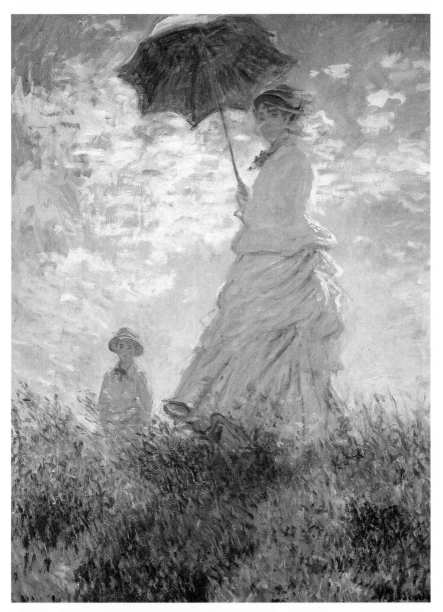

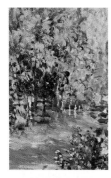

He liked to paint water, particularly the sea-coast near Le Havre, Trouville, Honfleur, and the Seine. He was drawn to views of Paris, the motifs of the garden and the forest road; while his groups of massive trees with clearings and buildings in the foreground were a tribute to the past, a link with the Barbizon group and Courbet, in the choice of motif at least.

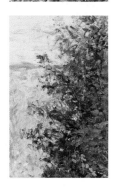

Corner of the Garden
at Montgeron

———————

1876-1877
oil on canvas, 173 x 192 cm
The Hermitage, Saint Petersburg

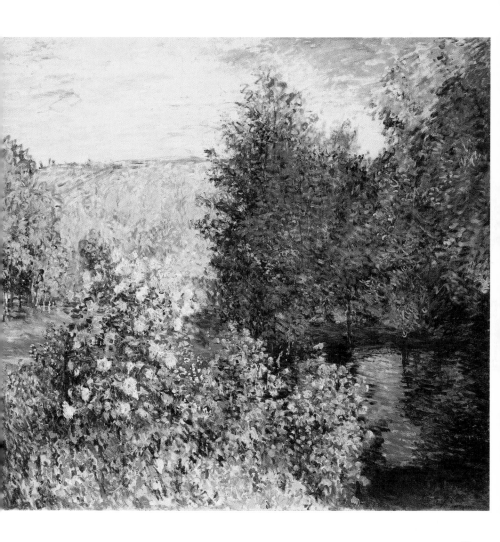

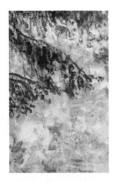

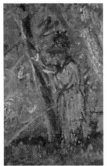

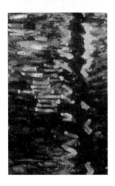

For Monet, as for every artist at the beginning of his career, the problem of his public, "his" viewer, was very acute. From the outset, painting was his sole source of income and he had to be able to sell his works. And no matter how creatively independent an artist might be, no matter how bold his ideas, the only way for him to attract attention was to exhibit at the official Salon.

The Pond at Montgeron

1876-1877
oil on canvas, 172 x 193 cm
The Hermitage, Saint Petersburg

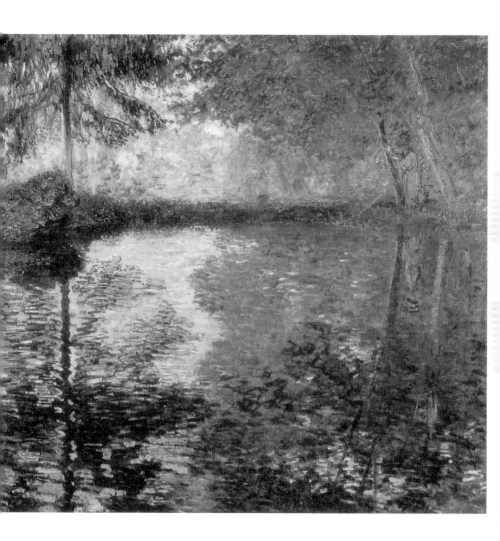

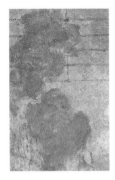

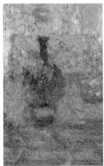

The Salon des Refusés held in opposition to the official Salon in 1863 had no successor during the Second Empire. Monet's first attempt to exhibit at the Salon was made in 1865 when he submitted two landscapes for the jury's consideration, *The Mouth of the Seine at Honfleur* (Norton Simon Foundation,

The Saint-Lazare Station

1877
oil on canvas, 75 x 100 cm
Musée d'Orsay, Paris

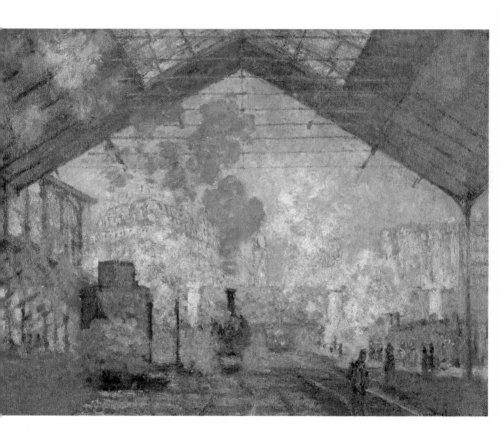

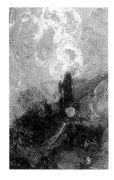

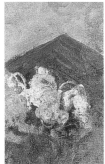

Los Angeles) and *Pointe de la Hève* (Kimbell Art Museum, Fort Worth, Texas). Both paintings were accepted and several of the critics, including the authoritative Paul Mantz, reacted positively towards them. This situation was repeated in 1866, although it was not the landscape, *The Road to Chailly in Fontainebleau* that attracted the attention of the critics this time,

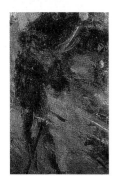

The Railway at the Exit
of Saint-Lazare Station

—————————————

1877
oil on canvas, 60 x 80 cm
private collection, Japan

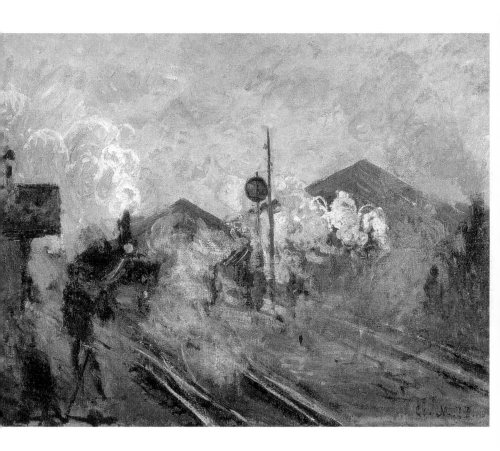

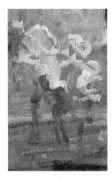

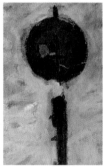

but the portrait given a genre painting treatment, *Woman in a Green Dress (Camille)*. In the following year, however, he suffered a reverse — the jury admitted only one of his landscapes. Such a turn of events was familiar to many innovative young painters in the nineteenth century. At first their paintings were accepted: no particularly daring features were discerned in them and the jury was demonstrating its liberalism.

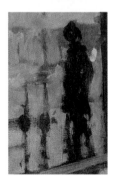

The Saint-Lazare Station, Outside

1877
oil on canvas, 65 x 81.5 cm
Niedersächsisches Landesmuseum, Hanover

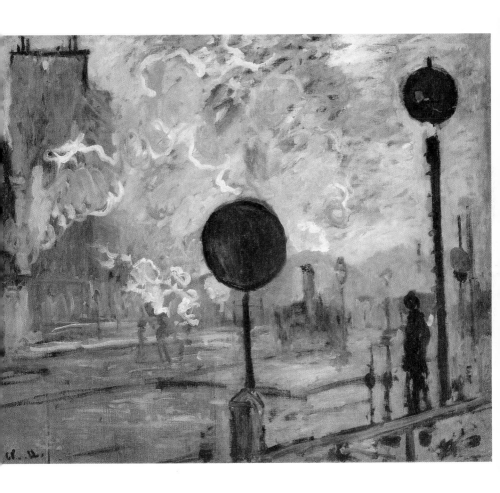

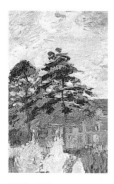

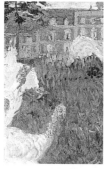

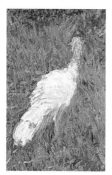

Then, as the painter's creative individuality and non-traditional, fresh view of the world became apparent, the jury became more guarded and the barriers went up. The late 1860s and early 1870s were an extremely important phase in Monet's career.

Turkeys
(Castle of Rottembourg at Montgeron)

1877
oil on canvas, 174,5 x 172,5 cm
Musée d'Orsay, Paris

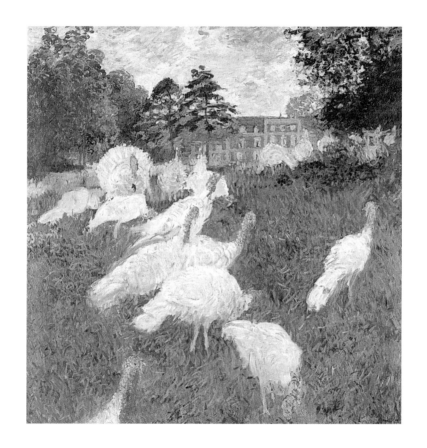

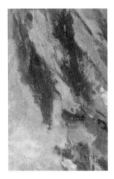

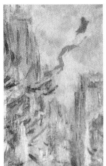

It is in his works from this period that the hand of an independent, innovative master began to be felt rather than that of a bold beginner. Alas, few people were aware of his achievements; all Monet's attempts to exhibit officially, be it at the Royal Academy in London in 1871 or at the Paris Salons of 1871 and 1873, met with failure.

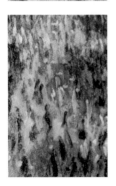

Rue Montorgueil
June 30th 1878 Celebration

1878
oil on canvas, 80 x 48.5 cm
Musée d'Orsay, Paris

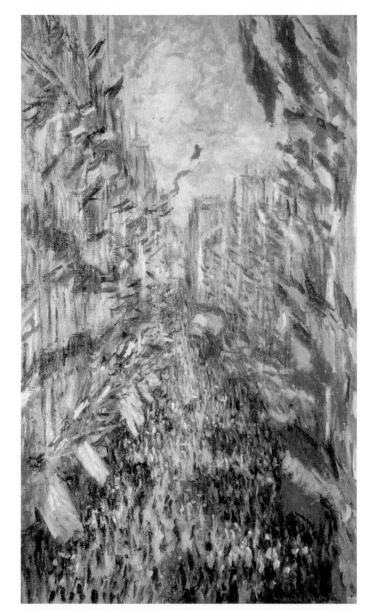

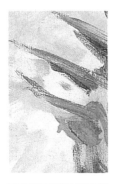

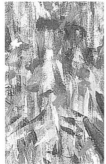

When commenting on Monet's work, many art scholars attach great significance to his visits in England and Holland in 1871, and to his first-hand acquaintance with the works of Constable and Turner. Yet without denying the influence of the English school of painting on Monet, its significance should certainly not be overestimated.

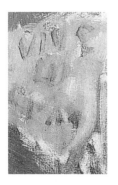

Rue Saint-Denis
30th 1878 Celebration

———————————

1878
oil on canvas, 76 x 52 cm
Musée des Beaux-Arts et de la Céramique, Rouen, France

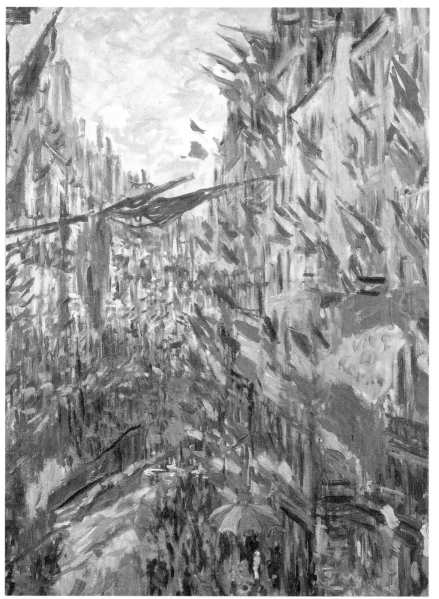

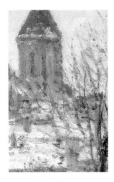

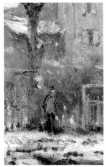

Working *en plein air*, he wanted to be an explorer who would be taught a new way of seeing by Nature herself, and Nature did indeed teach him. Returning to France, Monet felt the wealth and beauty of his own native countryside with unusual acuteness —

Snow Effects in Vétheuil
or Church in Vétheuil, Snow

1878-1879
oil on canvas, 52 x 71 cm
Musée d'Orsay, Paris

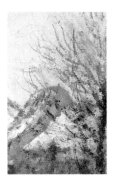

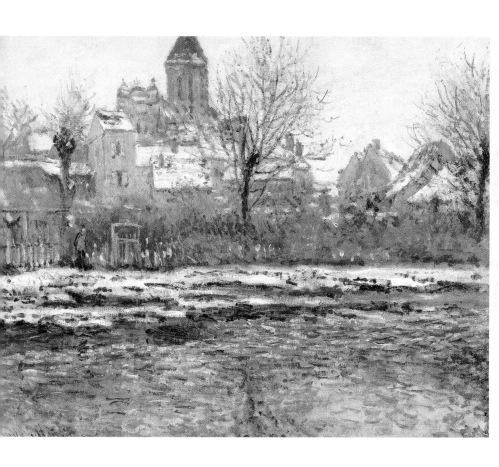

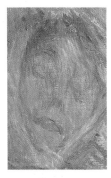

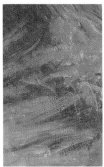

separation almost always sharpens one's perceptions and, quite naturally, the country-side of Normandy and the Ile-de-France with which his whole life was associated became not merely an object of study for him, but also of worship.

Camille on Her Deathbed

1879
oil on canvas, 90 x 68 cm
Musée d'Orsay, Paris

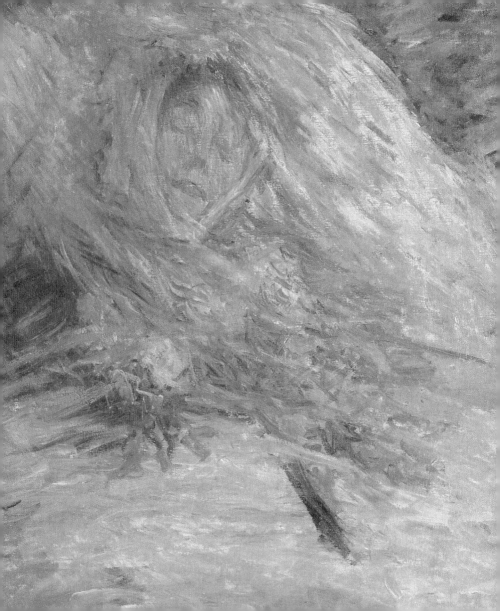

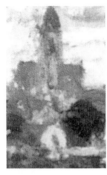

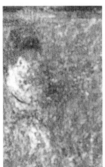

It was with a kind of rapture that he immersed himself in it, giving himself up totally to the creative impulse, and the canvases he produced in this state ring out like a hymn to the Nature of his native land.

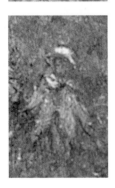

The Poppy Field near Vétheuil

1879
oil on canvas

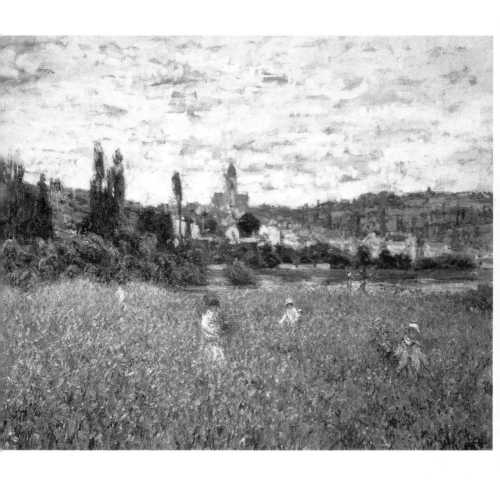

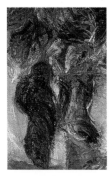

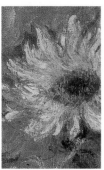

The year 1874 was an important date in the history of French art, for it was then that the country's rejected artists began their struggle for recognition, for the right to mount their own exhibitions and make contact with a public whom they would seek to draw towards their ideals and principles, rather than being at the mercy of its tastes and demands.

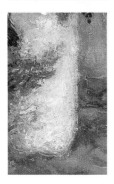

Bunch of Sunflowers

—————————————

1880
oil on canvas, 101 x 81.5 cm
The Metropolitan Museum of Art
New York

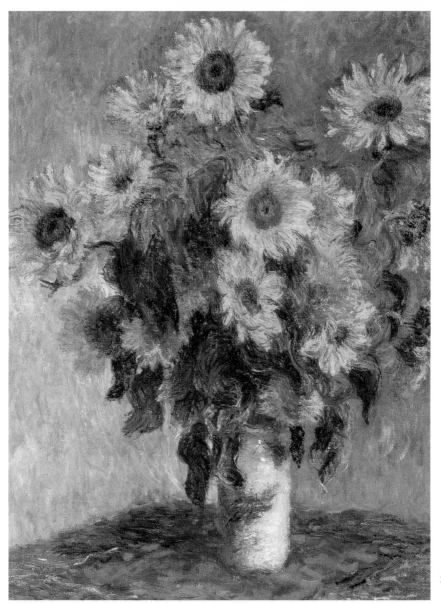

101

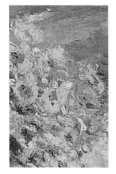

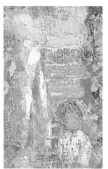

This struggle was unparalleled, for in the entire history of French art up to the appearance of the Impressionists there had actually been no group exhibitions outside the Salon. The Romantics in the 1820s and '30s, and the Realists in the mid-century, for all their shared ideological and aesthetic aims, had never formed new organizations to oppose the existing art establishment.

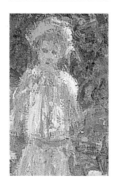

Monet's Garden in Vétheuil

1881
oil on canvas, 150 x 120 cm
National Gallery of Art
Washington (DC)

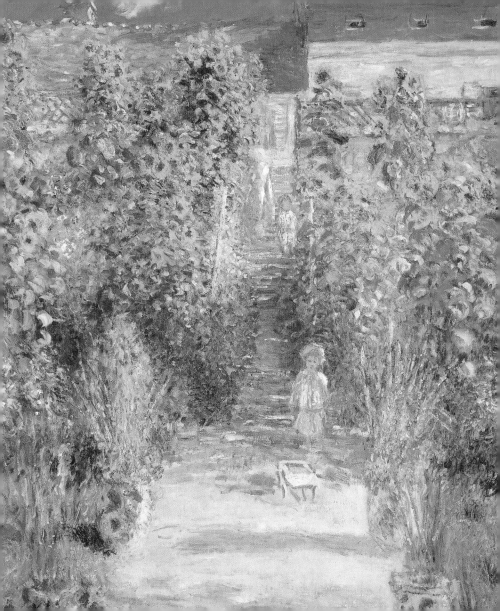

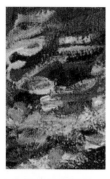

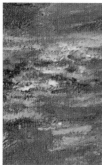

Even the Impressionists' immediate prede-
cessors in the sphere of landscape painting, the
Barbizon school painters, although so close to
one another both in their lives and in their work,
never arranged joint exhibitions.

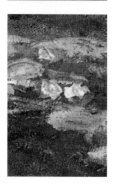

Water-Lilies Pond
_____

1917-1919
oil on canvas, 130 x 200 cm
The Art Institute of Chicago, Chicago

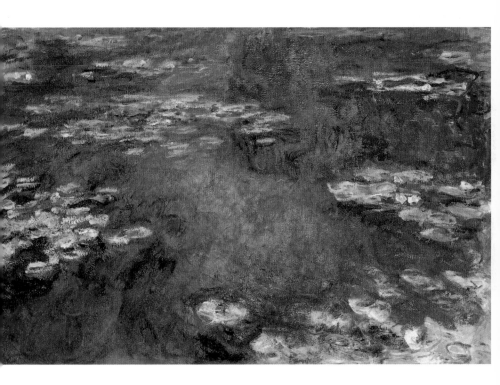

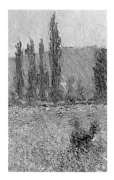

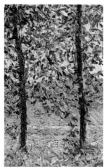

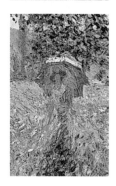

The Impressionists were pioneers breaking down established traditions, and Monet, as always, was in the forefront. The First Impressionist Exhibition opened on April 15th, 1874, at 35 Boulevard des Capucines.

Under the Poplars, Sunlight Effect

1887
oil on canvas
Staatsgalerie, Stuttgart

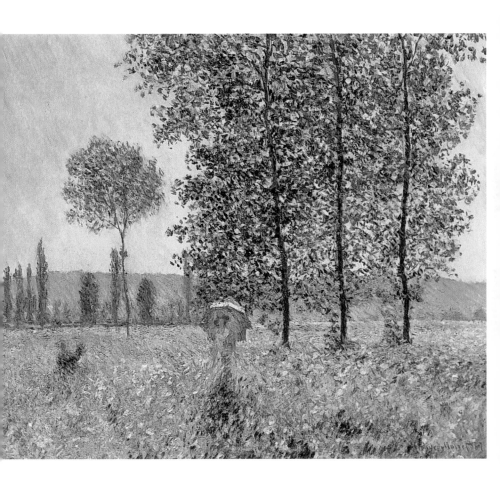

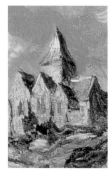

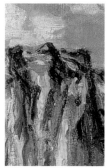

Thirty participants contributed 160 works, Monet providing nine, Renoir seven, Pissarro and Sisley five each, Degas ten, and Berthe Morisot nine. The artists exhibited oils, pastels and watercolours — of Monet's works, four were pastels.

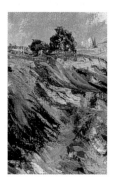

The Varangeville Church
Morning Effect

—————

1882
oil on canvas, 60 x 73 cm
private collection

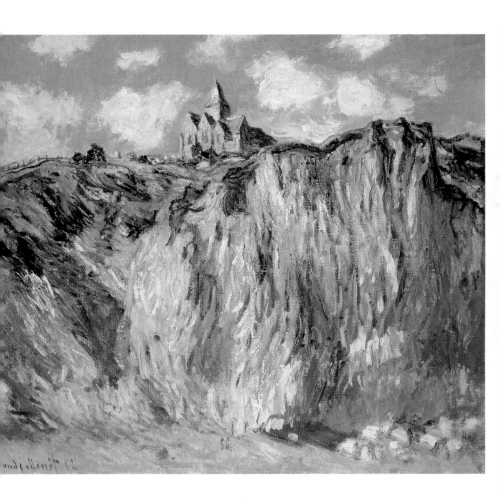

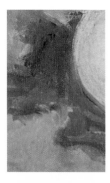

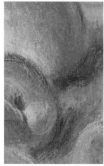

In the future his contributions would increase in number: for the second exhibition (1876) he provided eighteen works, for the third (1877) thirty, and for the fourth (1879) twenty-nine. He took no part in the fifth (1880) and sixth (1881) shows, but sent thirty-five pictures to the seventh in 1882, and was absent from the eighth.

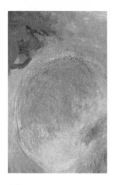

Peaches

———

1883
oil on canvas, 50.5 x 37 cm
private collection

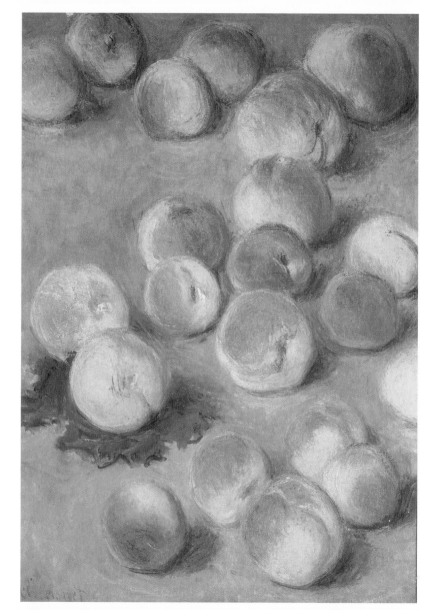

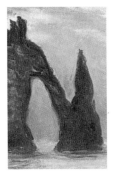

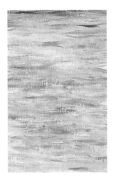

The importance of any given artist's contribution lay, of course, not only in the number of works exhibited. Their artistic merits, programmatic qualities and conformity to the aesthetic principles of the new movement were vital. In these respects Monet was invariably among the leading figures.

Etretat, Sunset

———————

1883
oil on canvas, 55 x 81 cm
North Carolina Museum of Art
Raleigh, North Carolina

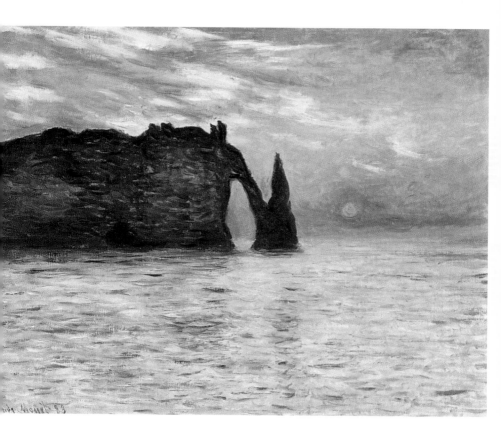

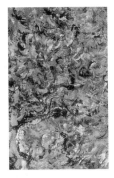

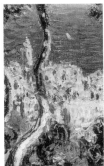

At the group's first exhibition viewers saw *The Luncheon,* rejected by the Salon jury in 1868; *Boulevard des Capucines* (1873), which now hangs in the Pushkin Museum of Fine Arts, Moscow; and the landscape painted at Le Havre in 1872, *Impression. Sunrise (Impression, soleil levant,* Musée Marmottan, Paris).

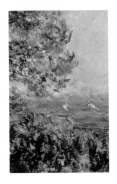

Bordighera

―――――

1884
oil on canvas, 65 x 81 cm
The Art Institute of Chicago

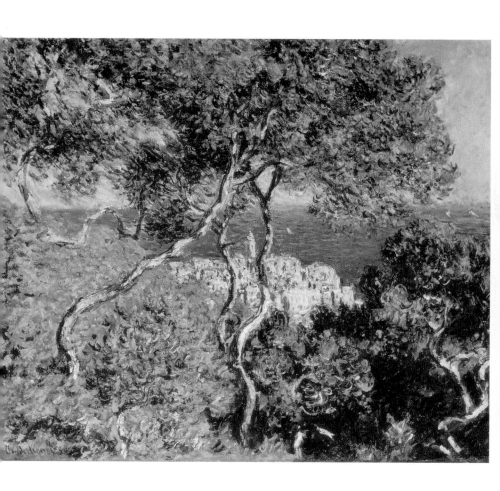

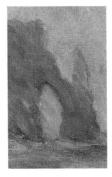

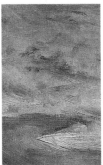

It was this latter painting that gave Louis Leroy, a critic from the magazine *Charivari*, occasion in his satirical review to dub the participants in the exhibition "Impressionists". Fate decided that a word thrown at the group in mockery should stick, and the artists themselves, although at first taking the name "Impressionist" as an insult, soon accepted it and grew to love it.

Etretat, The Rain

––––––––––––––

1885-1886
oil on canvas, 60.5 x 73.5 cm
Nasionalgalleriet, Oslo

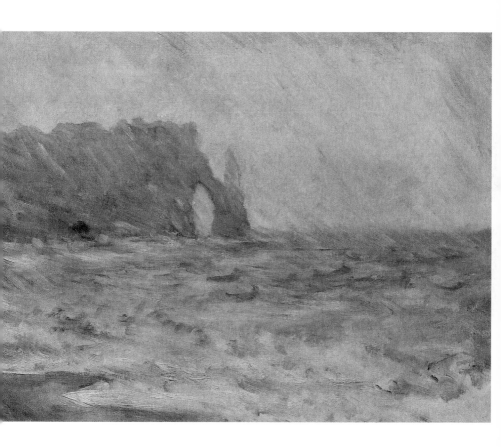

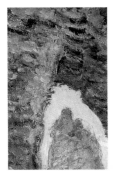

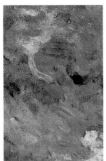

Monet's *Le Havre* landscape corresponded precisely with the essentials of the movement which would be termed "Impressionism" in the 1880s and 1890s by French critics, and eventually by the critics and art historians of all other countries too.

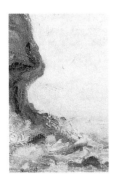

The Rock Needle
through the Porte d'Aval

1885-1886
oil on canvas, 73 x 92 cm
private collection, USA

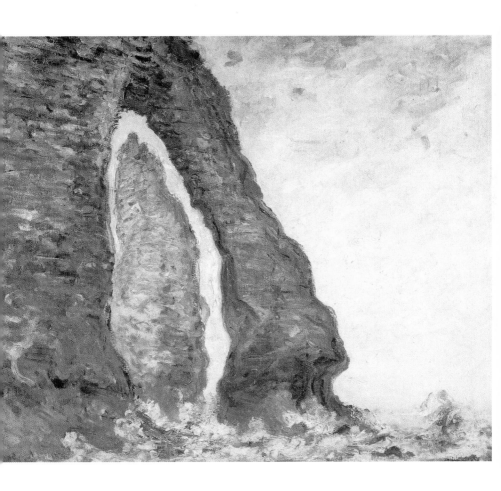

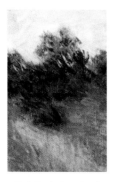

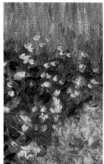

The picture *Boulevard des Capucines* is no less programmatic, this time demonstrating the Impressionist interpretation of the motif of the city. The artist is looking at the Boulevard from an elevated viewpoint, the balcony of Nadar's studio on the corner of the Boulevard des Capucines and Rue Daunou.

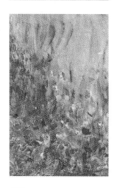

The Poppy Field, near Giverny

1885
oil on canvas, 65 x 81 cm
Museum of Fine Arts, Boston, Massachusetts

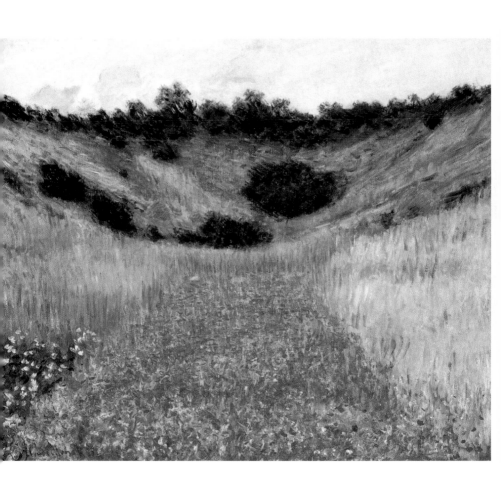

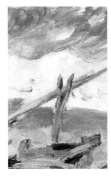

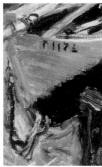

He even brings the figures of men on the balcony into the composition, seeming to invite the viewer to stand alongside them and admire the unfolding spectacle. The Boulevard stretches into the distance towards the Opera, pedestrians hurry along, carriages pass by,

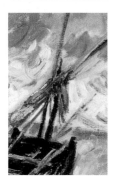

Three Fishing Boats

1885
oil on canvas
Budapest

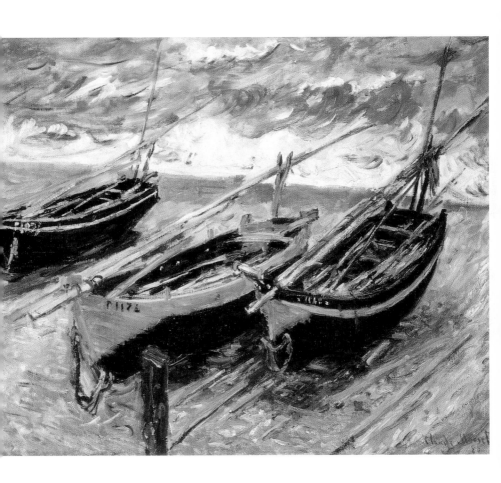

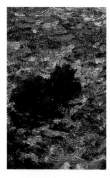

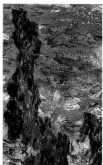

shadows move across the walls of buildings, and rays of sunlight, breaking through the storm-clouds, sparkle, colouring all in warm, golden tones… Monet gives no attention whatsoever to individual buildings, even those of note (as he did in an early cityscape showing the church of

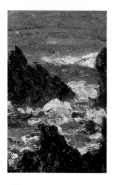

The Rocks at Belle-Ile

1886
oil on canvas, 65 x 81 cm
The Pushkin Museum of Fine Arts, Moscow

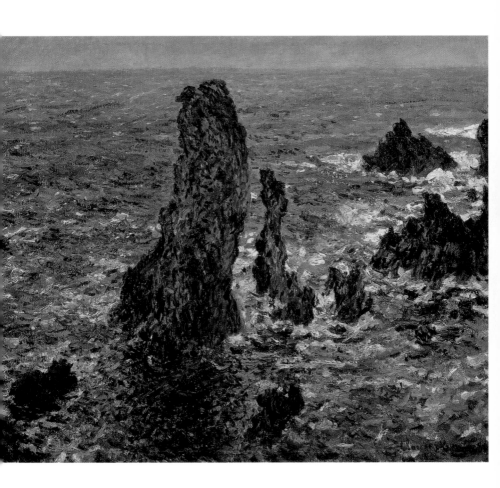

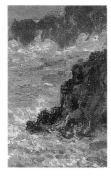

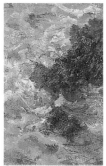

St. Germain-l'Auxerrois in Paris): the city interests him as a unified, mobile organism in which every detail is linked to another. At first hesitantly, and then with increasing freedom and confidence, Monet developed his manner of painting to correspond with his altered artistic perception.

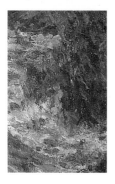

The Rocks at Belle-Ile

1886
oil on canvas, 65 x 81.5 cm
Musée d'Orsay, Paris

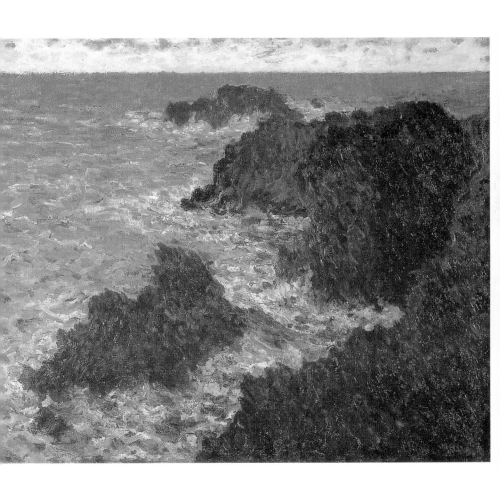

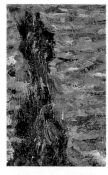

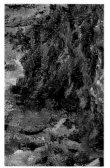

In this sense, in the 1870s he achieved perfect balance and harmony. At the Second Impressionist Exhibition Monet displayed landscapes, for the most part of Argenteuil, and the figure composition *La Japonaise* (1875, Museum of Fine Art, Boston).

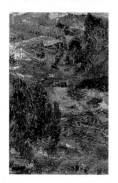

The Rock Needle of Porte-Coton

sale, Sotheby, November 29, 1972, London

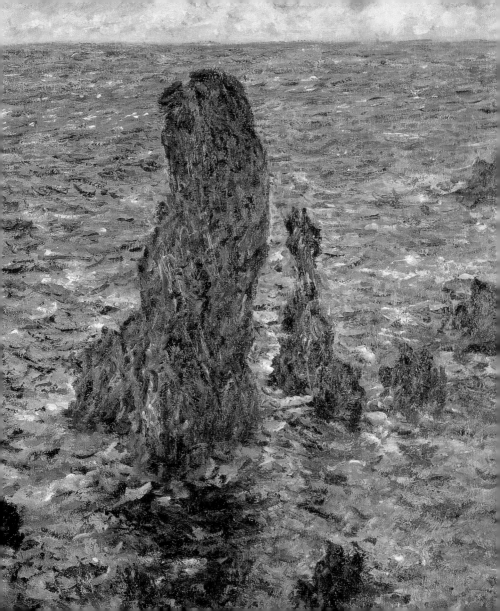

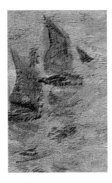

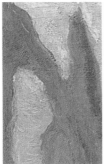

If *La Japonaise,* which depicted the artist's wife, Camille, in a kimono, still tended towards Monet's "old" style, the paint being laid on thickly in broad strokes, the landscapes on the contrary continued the trend indicated by the views of Le Havre in the early 1870s,

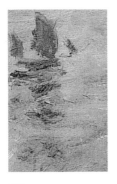

The Rocks at Etretat

1886
oil on canvas, 66 x 81 cm
The Pushkin Museum of Fine Arts, Moscow

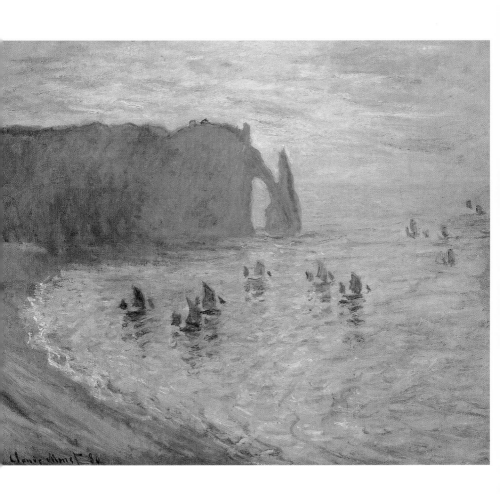

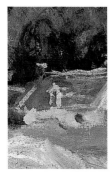

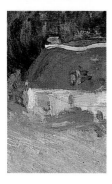

the *Boulevard des Capucines* and other works in a similar vein. From 1872 onwards Monet lived mainly at Argenteuil, a small town on the Seine not far from Paris. Other artists came to visit him there, as though to underline his outstanding role in the establishment of Impressionism.

Haystack at Giverny
_____

1886
oil on canvas, 61 x 81 cm
The Hermitage, Saint Petersburg

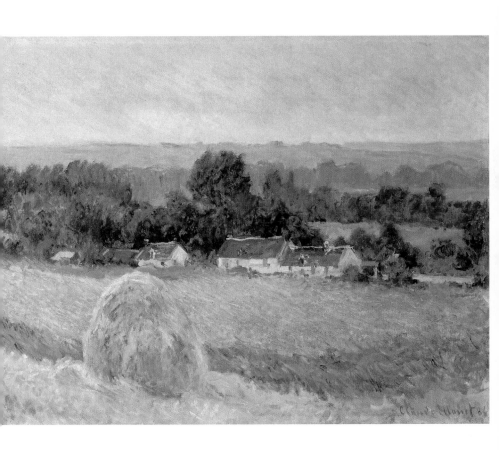

133

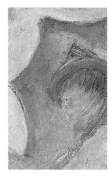

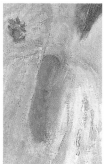

Among them was Manet, who in 1874 painted such well-known pictures as *Argenteuil, Boating; On the Bank of the Seine; Claude Monet in his Studio Boat* and others. Edouard Manet consistently singled Monet out from the other Impressionists, and in his reminiscences Antonin Proust recalls the elder artist's words about his younger colleague:

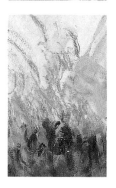

Sketch for a Figure in Open Air
(to the left)

———

1886
oil on canvas, 131 x 88 cm
Musée d'Orsay, Paris

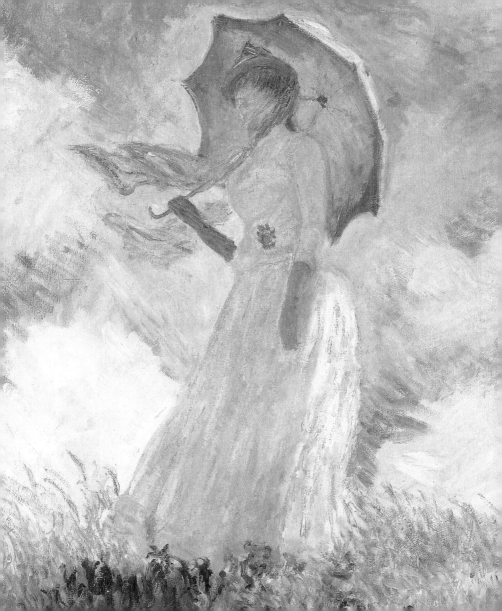

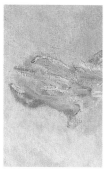

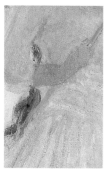

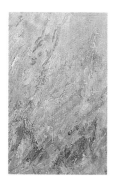

"In the entire school of the '30s there is no one who could paint landscape like that. And his water! He is the Raphael of water. He feels its every movement, all its depth, all its variations at different times of the day."

Sketch for a Figure in Open Air
(to the right)

———————

1886
oil on canvas, 131 x 88 cm
Musée d'Orsay, Paris

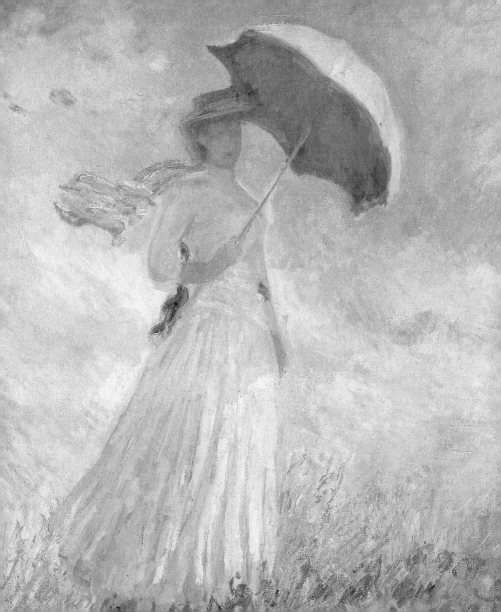

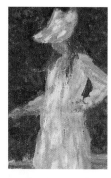

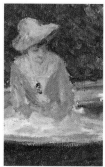

The foremost theme in Monet's work of the 1870s was Argenteuil. He painted the Seine with boats and without them, reflecting the resonant blue of the sky or leaden grey under wintry clouds. He enjoyed painting the town as well, now powdered with snow, now sunny and green.

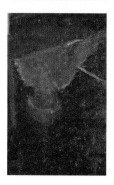

In the Row-Boat

1887
oil on canvas, 98 x 131 cm
Musée d'Orsay, Paris

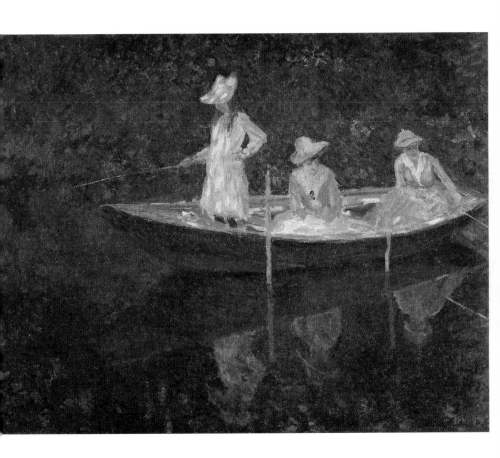

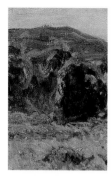

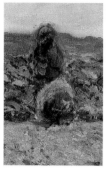

In fine weather he would go for walks in the environs of Argenteuil, sometimes with his wife and son, and these strolls gave rise to canvases filled with the intoxicating joy of living. One of these is *The Poppies* (*A Promenade*) (1873, Musée d'Orsay, Paris).

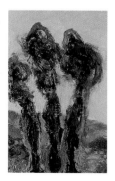

The Poppy Field

about 1887
oil on canvas, 59 x 60 cm
The Hermitage, Saint Petersburg

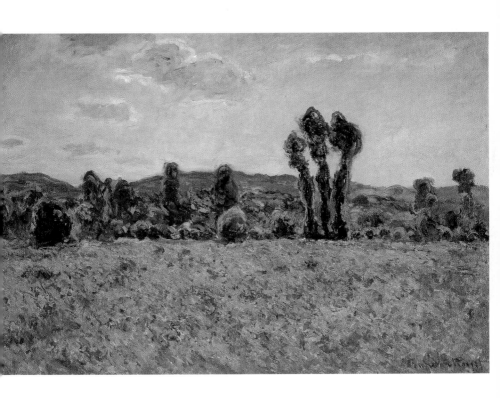

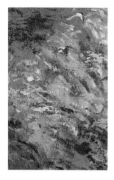

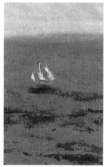

In his Argenteuil period Monet shows a preference for landscapes that convey wide expanses of space with an uncluttered foreground. This sort of composition lends paintings a panoramic quality, space being developed in breadth rather than in depth,

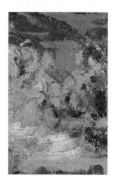

At the Cape of Antibes with Mistral

1888
oil on canvas, 65 x 81 cm
Museum of Fine Arts, Boston, Massachusetts

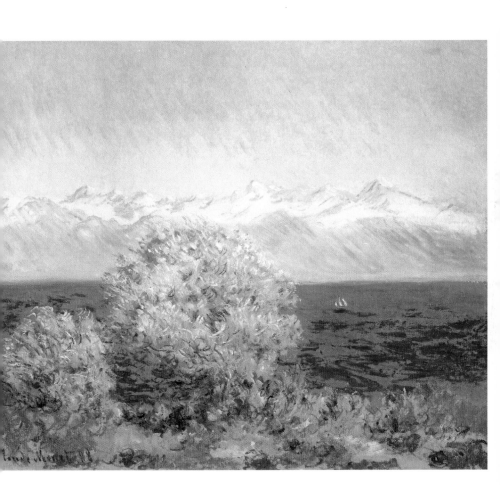

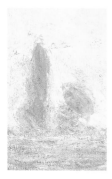

with horizontals expressed by rivers, riverbanks, lines of houses, groups of trees, the sails of yachts turned parallel to the surface of the canvas and so on. The dynamics of the life of Nature are captured by Monet in the Argenteuil cycle both in minor, everyday phenomena and at crucial moments.

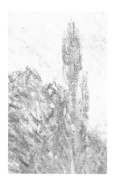

Meadows at Giverny

1888
oil on canvas, 92 x 80 cm
The Hermitage, Saint Petersburg

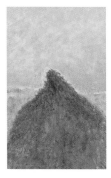

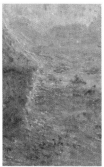

When Monet was in Paris he could most often be found in his favourite district on the right bank near the railway station of Saint-Lazare. These were familiar haunts for Monet, as he used to arrive here from Le Havre and leave from here when travelling out into the environs of Paris.

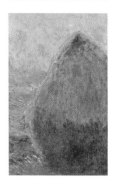

Haystacks at Giverny
in Muted Sunlight
──────────────
1888-1889
oil on canvas, 65 x 92 cm
Saitama Museum of Modern Art, Urawa-shi

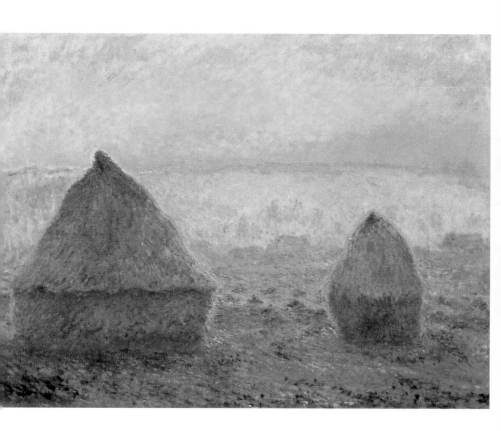

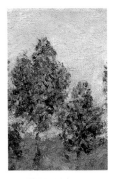

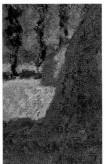

He covered canvas after canvas here, creating in the first cycle of his career *La Gare Saint-Lazare* (1877). The theme of the railway was not a new one in European art. The views of Saint-Lazare station and his landscapes of Montgeron were Monet's major contributions to the Third Impressionist Exhibition, but neither the public nor the critics took them seriously.

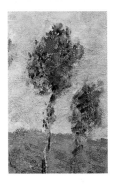

Haystack near Giverny

1889
oil on canvas, 64.5 x 81 cm
The Pushkin Museum of Fine Arts, Moscow

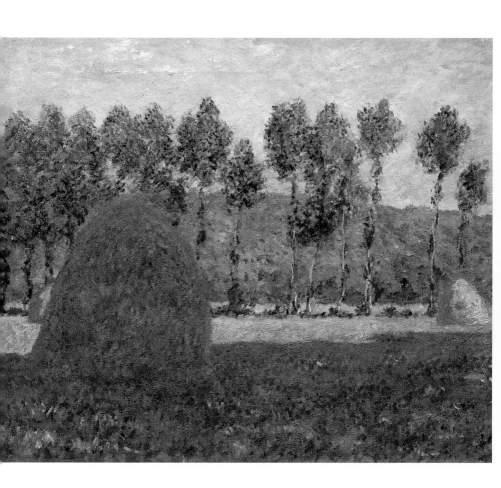

149

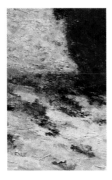

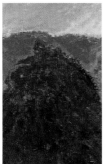

Of *Turkeys*, one of the decorative Mont-geron canvases distinguished by its marvel-lously rhythmic structure, it was written that Monet had simply scattered white blobs with necks attached on a green background, that the painting lacked air and that as a whole it created a ridiculous impression.

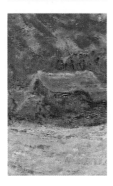

Haystack, Effect of Snow, Cloudy Weather

1890-1891
oil on canvas, 65 x 92 cm
The Art Institute of Chicago
Collection Mr and Mrs Martin A. Ryerson, Chicago

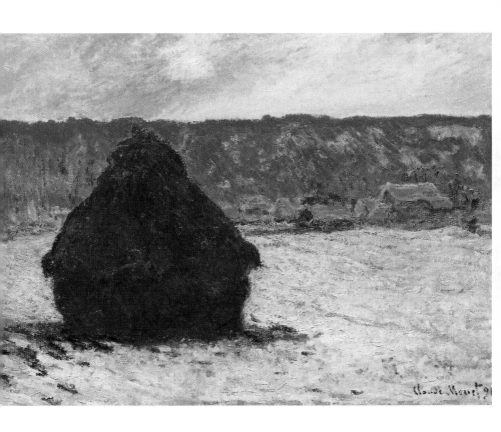

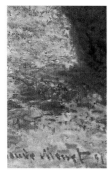

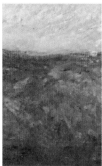

The fourth Exhibition was somewhat less varied, for Renoir, Sisley and Berthe Morisot were all absent. However, the contributions from Monet and Pissarro continued to affirm the central role of the landscape in the Impressionist movement.

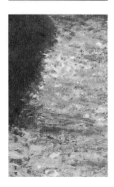

Haystack, Thaw, Sunset
_____

1890-1891
oil on canvas, 65 x 92 cm
The Art Institute of Chicago, Chicago

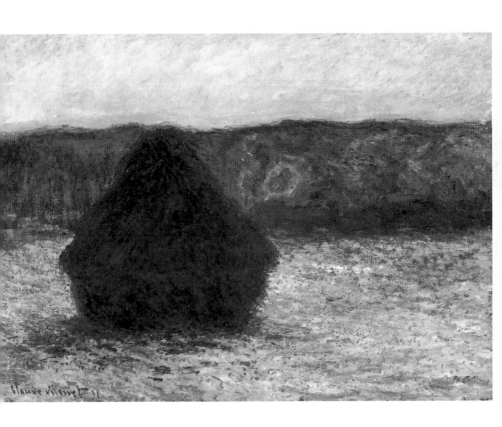

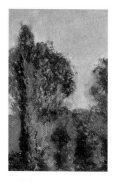

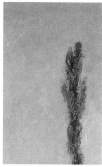

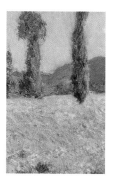

The main attacks from the critics were provoked by Monet's *La Rue Montorgueuil, June 30, 1878* (1878, private collection, Paris) and *La Rue Saint-Denis, June 30, 1878* (1878, Musée des Beaux-Arts, Rouen).

Poppy Field

———————

1890
oil on canvas, 65 x 92 cm
The Art Institute of Chicago
Collection Mr and Mrs W.W. Kimball, Chicago

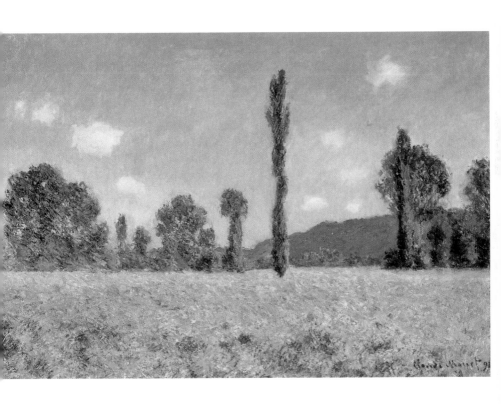

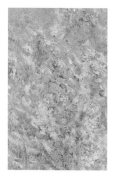

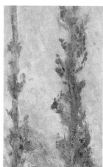

The cityscapes shown by Monet at the fourth exhibition reveal changes in his treatment of the urban theme and changes in his style as a whole. The streets of Montorgueuil and St. Denis had been decorated for the World Fair.

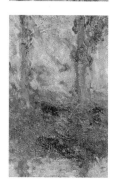

Poplars, White and Yellow Effects

1891
oil on canvas, 100 x 65 cm
The Philadelphia Museum of Art
Chester Dale Collection, Philadelphia, Pennsylvania

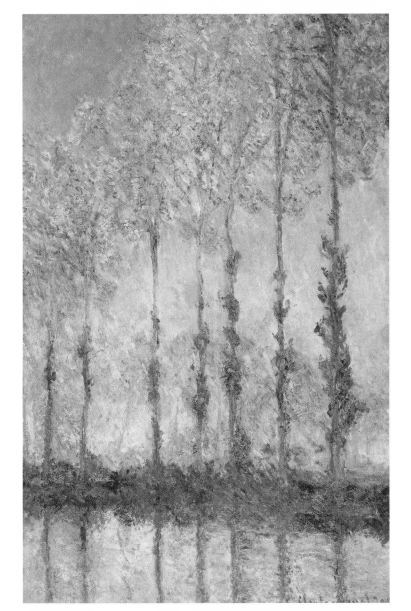

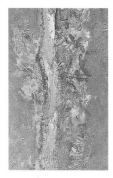

To produce the paintings, Monet adopted a viewpoint similar to the one he had chosen for the *Boulevard des Capucines,* looking down from a balcony, only now the compositions gave no indication of the position from which the pictures were painted.

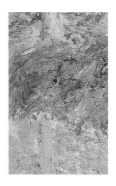

Poplars, Three Pink Trees, Autumn

1891
oil on canvas, 92 x 73 cm
The Philadelphia Museum of Art
Chester Dale Collection, Philadelphia, Pennsylvania

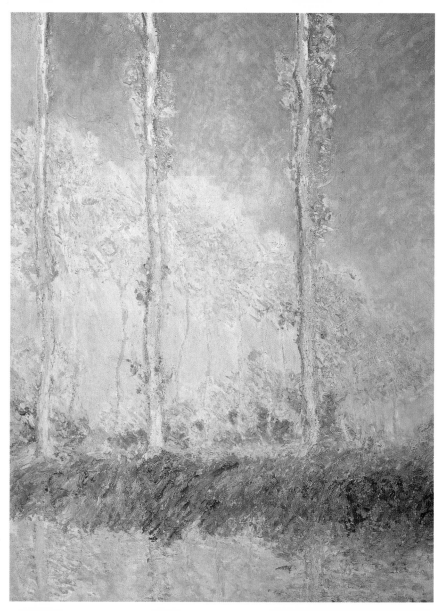

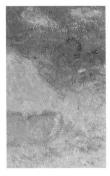

The views of the Saint-Lazare Station displayed new developments in the character of Monet's painting. It is painted with powerful brushstrokes which at times "fragment" the object being depicted. Similarly, in *Flags* the comma-like strokes have become frenzied;

Haystacks, End of an Autumn Day

1891
oil on canvas, 65 x 100 cm
The Art Institute of Chicago
Mr and Mrs Lewis Larned Coburn Memorial
Collection, Chicago

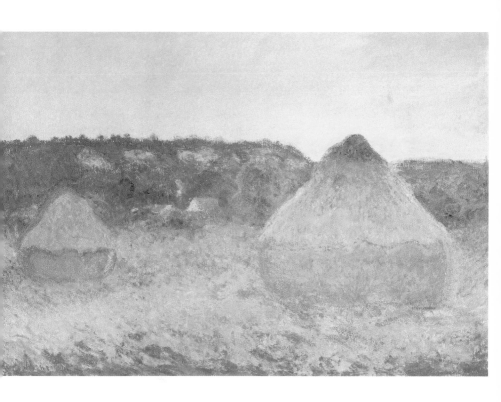

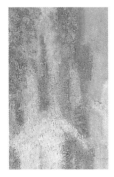

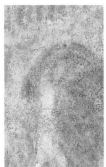

energetic marks of the brush literally lash the surface of the canvas, and the colours, especially the various shades of red, ring out loudly and confidently. Always preoccupied with the problems of rendering light and air, Monet had thus by the late 1870s or early 1880s achieved a heightened expressiveness of colour and a powerful and dynamic brushstroke.

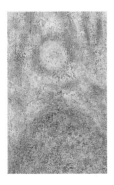

Rouen Cathedral
Grey and Pink Symphony

1892
oil on canvas, 100 x 65 cm
National Museum of Wales, Cardiff, England

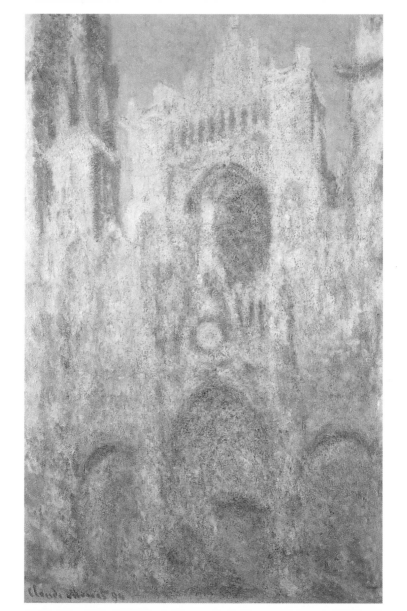

Claude Monet 94

163

In 1880, Monet was forty years old. The Impressionists, and Monet more than anyone, wanted to transform Nature herself into a workshop and to erase the distinction between the sketch, the result of direct observation, and the picture, the synthesis of the whole creative process.

The Portal, Morning Fog

1893
oil on canvas, 100 x 65 cm
Museum Folkwang, Essen

Claude Monet 94

165

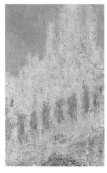

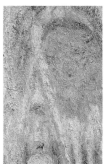

Thus Monet's correspondence abounds in complaints about changes in the weather. He is brought to despair by rain, winds and inconsistent light, all of which hamper his work, and yet at the same time it is Nature's very changeability that is so attractive to him.

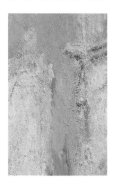

Rouen Cathedral in the Evening
_____

1894
oil on canvas, 100 x 65 cm
The Pushkin Museum of Fine Arts, Moscow

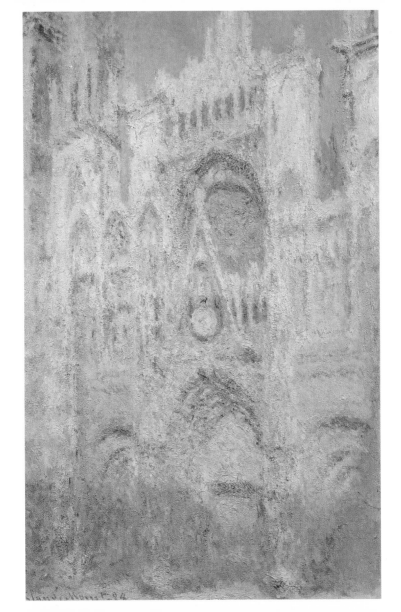

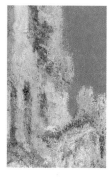

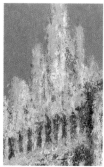

How can one convey by means of paint the grass swaying in the wind or the ripples on the surface of water? How can one transfer onto canvas the fluffiness of newly-fallen snow or the crackling fragility of melting ice as it flows downstream?

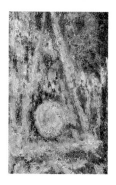

Rouen Cathedral, Portal of
Saint-Romain's Tower (Full Sun)

1894
oil on canvas, 107 x 73 cm
Musée d'Orsay, Paris

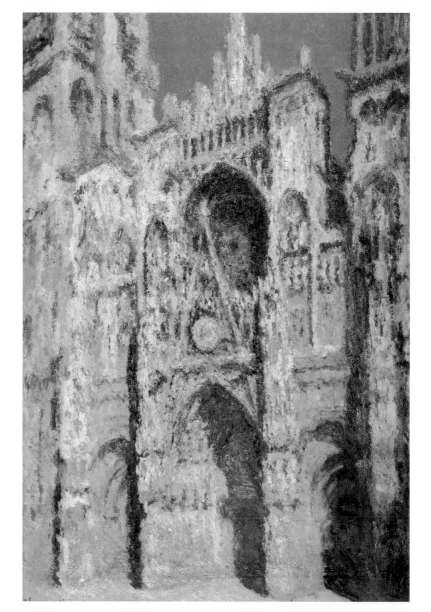

169

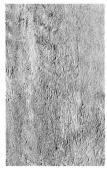

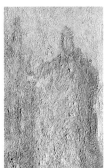

It was Monet's firm conviction that all this can be achieved by tireless observation and so, dressed in comfortable clothing suitable to the weather, the artist would go out to work every day, morning, afternoon and evening.

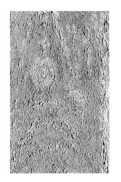

Rouen Cathedral at Noon

1894
oil on canvas, 101 x 65 cm
The Pushkin Museum of Fine Arts, Moscow

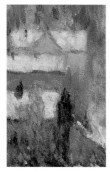

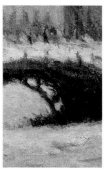

What were the tangible results of the decade that had just closed? How was Monet regarded by his contemporaries — not the friends and colleagues who were thrilled by his art, but the public, and the press which shaped public opinion?

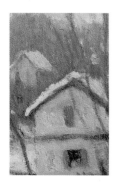

Winter Landscape (Sandviken)
_____

1895
oil on cardboard, 37 x 52.5 cm
The Latvian Republican Museum of Foreign Art, Riga

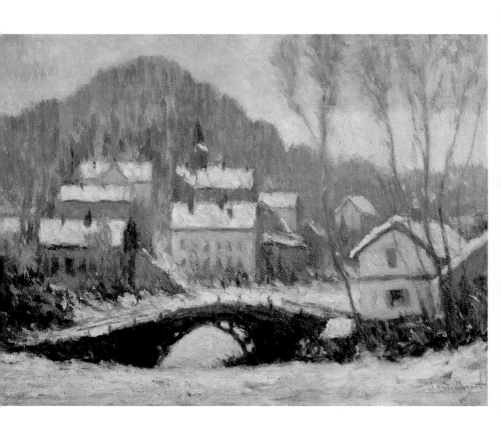

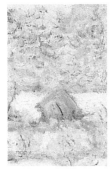

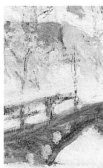

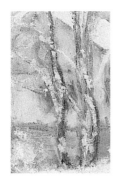

With rare exceptions, the critics spoke of Monet in the most disparaging terms. The situation of his family, then consisting of two children and a sick wife (Camille died in 1879 after a painful illness), was catastrophic indeed, as extracts from his letters attest.

Sandviken Village under the Snow

1895
oil on canvas, 73 x 92 cm
The Art Institute of Chicago

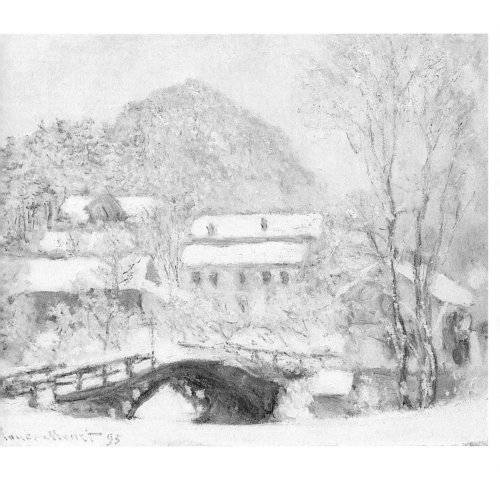

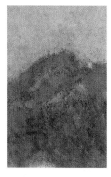

After spending several years at Vétheuil on the Seine, Monet settled down in 1883 at Giverny, henceforth his main place of residence, although he did a good deal of travelling in the 1880s. In the spring of 1883 he worked on the Normandy coast, at Le Havre and Etretat, and in December of that year he set out with Renoir for the Riviera.

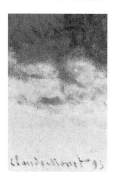

Kolsaas Mountain, Misty Weather

1895
oil on canvas, 65 x 100 cm
lent by Gay und Clifton Leonhardt
Cornell University, Ithaka, New York

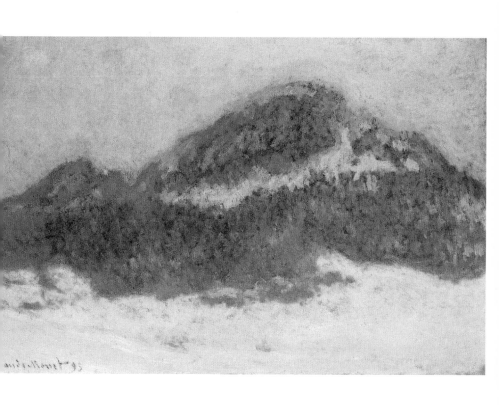

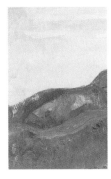

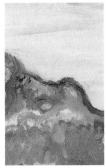

In 1884, after Bordighera and Menton, he returned to Etretat, where he also spent several months during the following summer. The year 1886 was memorable for trips to Holland and Brittany; from January to April 1888 he lived on the Mediterranean coast at Antibes, before moving on to London and thence back to Etretat.

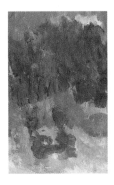

Kolsaas Mountain

1895
oil on canvas, 65 x 92 cm
private collection, USA

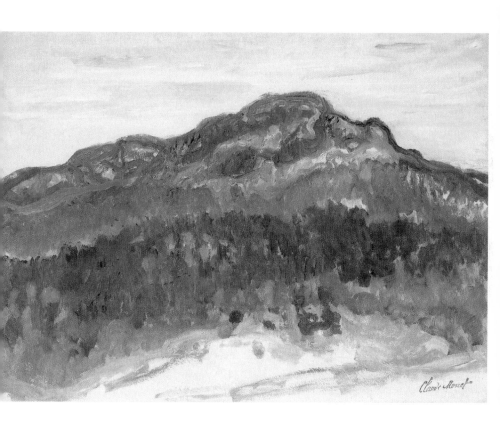

These journeys were undoubtedly efforts to find new sources for his work, new and inspiring motifs. Nevertheless, in all his wanderings, Monet remained resolutely faithful to the central principle of his art, trying to penetrate deep into Nature, to apprehend her secrets and convey them through vivid and direct perception.

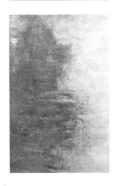

The Branch of the Seine at Giverny, Fog

1897
oil on canvas, 89 x 92 cm
North Carolina Museum of Art, Raleigh, North Carolina

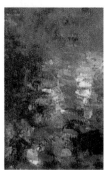

Alongside the landscapes of Normandy, Brittany and the Mediterranean, the motif of Giverny appears in Monet's work of the 1880s, returning the artist to the landscapes of the Ile-de-France so dear to his heart.

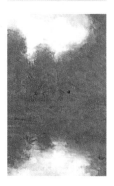

Morning on the Seine

1897
oil on canvas, 81 x 92 cm
private collection, USA

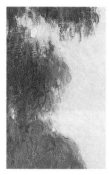

In fact he had never really parted with them, but they had become noticeably less frequent. Now, Monet was attracted by the expressiveness of strictly linear rhythms, and his treatment of form became increasingly a matter of planes.

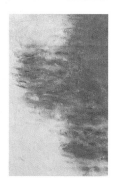

Branch of the Seine at Giverny, Daybreak

1897
oil on canvas, 81 x 92 cm
Hiroshima Museum of Art, Hiroshima

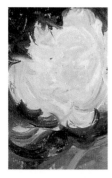

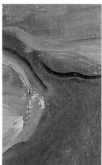

During the 1880s the feeling of a crisis was experienced in one way or another by all the creators of the Impressionist style; Pissarro, for example, became closer to Seurat and Signac, and turned sharply towards Divisionism, while Renoir felt a new enthusiasm for Ingres and the Renaissance masters.

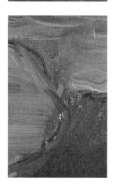

Water-Lilies

1897-1898
oil on canvas, 65 x 100 cm
Los Angeles County Museum of Art
Los Angeles

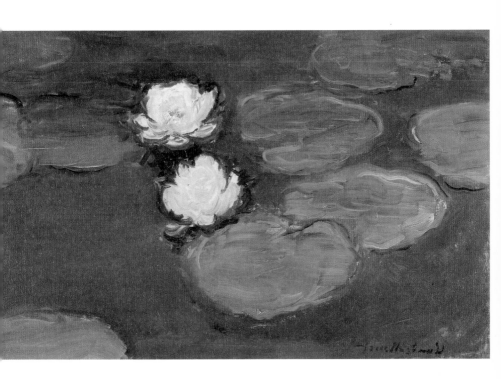

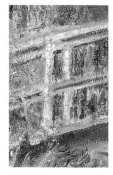

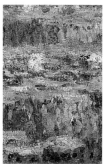

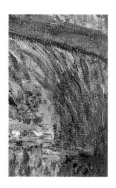

Unlike them, Monet did not turn towards any extraneous influence but rather followed the logic of his own artistic development, which drove him to a continual intensification of his own experimentation. This tendency had always been characteristic of Monet, but his perception of Nature as a unity had remained constant, always maintaining a harmonious equilibrium as he represented her particular characteristics.

Pond with Water-Lilies

1897-1899
oil on canvas, 90 x 90 cm
The Art Museum, Princeton University
Princeton, New Jersey

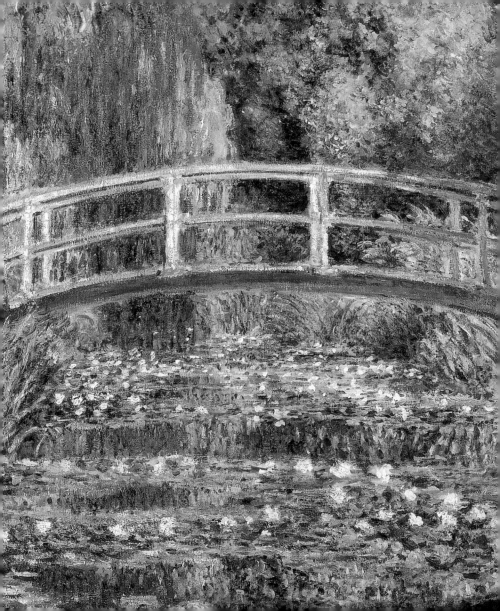

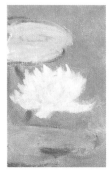

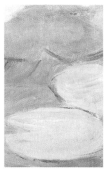

In the 1890s and 1900s, however, Monet's experiments with light and colour frequently became almost an end in themselves and, as a result, his harmonious perception of Nature began to disappear. It is indicative that during this period he was already working in isolation.

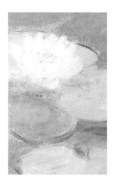

Pink Water-Lilies

1897-1899
oil on canvas, 81 x 100 cm
Galleria Nazionale d'Arte Moderna, Roma

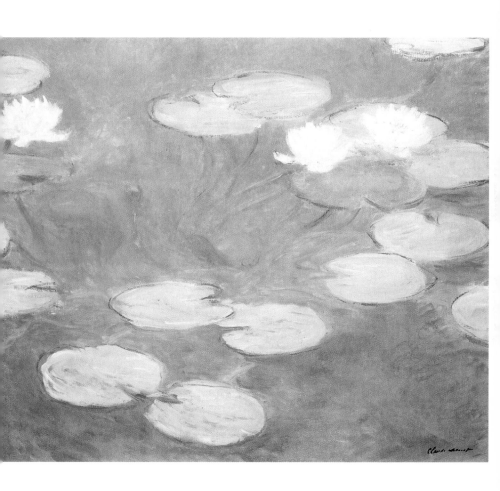

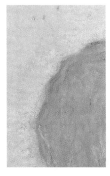

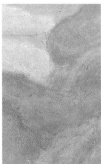

Although this did not mean breaking off personal contacts with the friends of his youth, creative contact with them was lost. There were no more joint exhibitions, no exchanges of opinion and no arguments. One of the central problems tackled by Monet at the end of the nineteenth and beginning of the twentieth century was that of serial work.

On the Cliffs near Dieppe

1897
oil on canvas, 64.5 x 100 cm
The Hermitage, Saint Petersburg

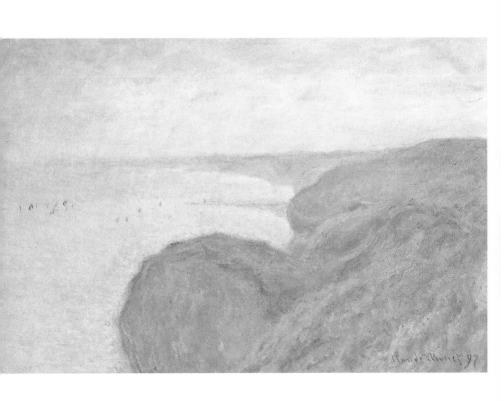

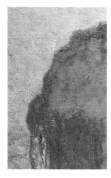

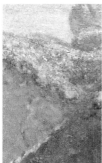

The principle of work in series had been used by artists before Monet, especially in the field of graphic art, with cycles of several sheets devoted to a single event, hero, town and so on. Artists were particularly prolific with series depicting the seasons of the year, some of them relying on the language of conventional allegory, others depicting rural labour at different times of the year.

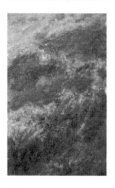

At the Val Saint-Nicolas
near Dieppe, in the Morning

1897
oil on canvas, 65 x 100 cm
The Phillips Collection, Washington, D.C

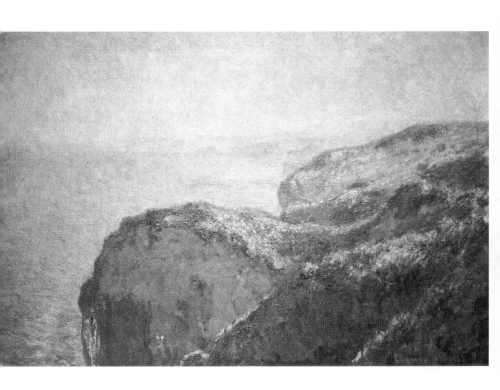

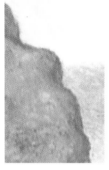

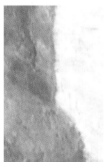

Before Monet, however, no one in European art had created series devoted to a single motif such as haystacks, a row of poplars, or the facade of a cathedral. Monet's forerunners in this respect were Japanese artists, in particular Katsushika Hokusai, the creator of numerous series, including the celebrated *36 Views of Mount Fuji*.

The Tip of the Petit Ailly
Cloudy Weather

1897
oil on canvas, 73 x 92 cm
private collection, USA

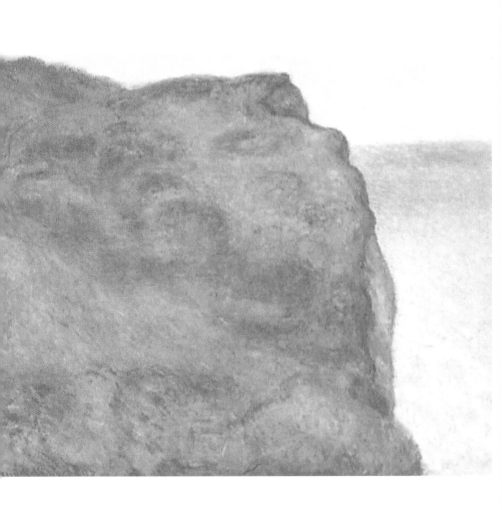

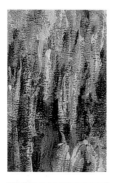

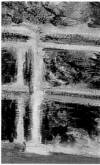

Throughout Monet's series the basic subject remains unchanged but the lighting varies. Thus as the eye becomes accustomed to looking at one and the same object, it gradually loses interest in the thing itself and, like the artist, the viewer is no longer attracted by the subject as such, but rather by the changing light playing on its surfaces.

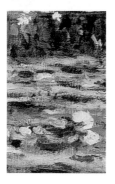

White Water-Lilies

———————

1899
oil on canvas, 89 x 93 cm
The Pushkin Museum of Fine Arts, Moscow

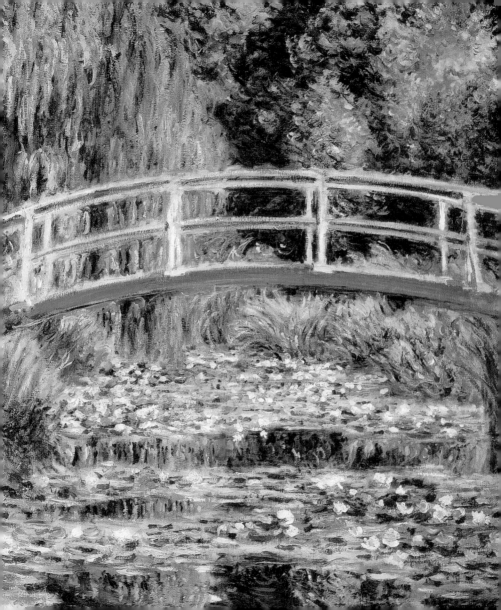

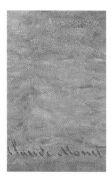

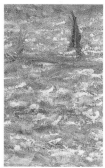

Hence it is light that becomes the "hero" of each painting, dictating its own laws, colouring objects in various ways, imparting either solidity or transparency, and altering contours by either rendering the boundaries of forms uncertain, or making them perceptible only as sharp silhouettes.

London, Waterloo Bridge

1899-1901
oil on canvas, 65 x 92 cm
Santa Barbara Museum of Art
Santa Barbara, California

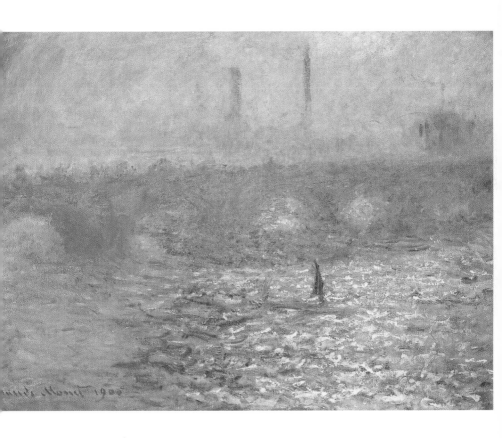

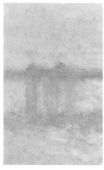

The idea of creating the *Rouen Cathedral* series came to Monet in 1892 while he was staying in Rouen, where, enchanted by the cathedral, he lived directly opposite to it. From the window of his room he could see, not the whole building, but only the portal, and this determined the composition of the canvases in the first part of the cycle.

Charing Cross Bridge
Cloudy Weather

———————

1899-1901
oil on canvas, 65 x 81 cm
Museum of Fine Arts, Boston, Massachusetts

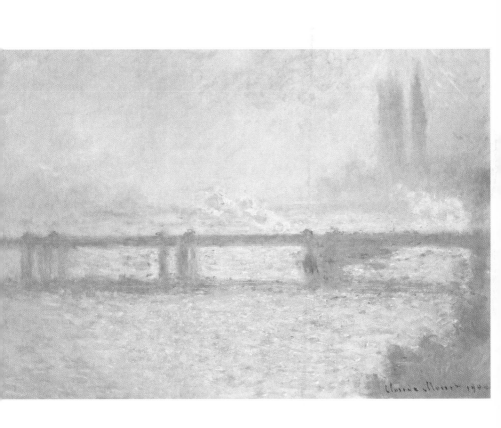

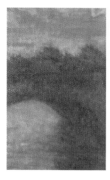

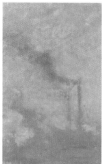

In these the artist's field of vision is invariably limited to the portal and the patch of sky above it. It is a "close-up" composition, with a part of the cathedral, transformed by the skilled hands of mason and sculptor into stone lacework, occupying the entire area of the canvas.

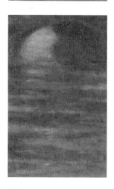

Waterloo Bridge
Cloudy Weather

1899-1901
oil on canvas, 65 x 100 cm
Hugh Lane Municipal Gallery of Modern Art, Dublin

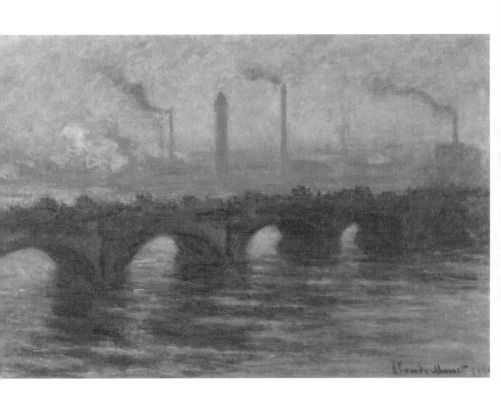

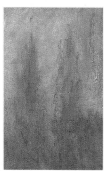

Previously, looking from a cliff, a hill or the window of a room, he liked to impart a sense of space by leaving the foreground free. Now the subject was approached almost at point-blank range, and yet its proximity did not help to elucidate its nature, for light reduced it to next to nothing.

The Houses of Parliament, Sunset

1900-1901
oil on canvas, 81 x 92 cm,
The Brooklyn Museum, New York

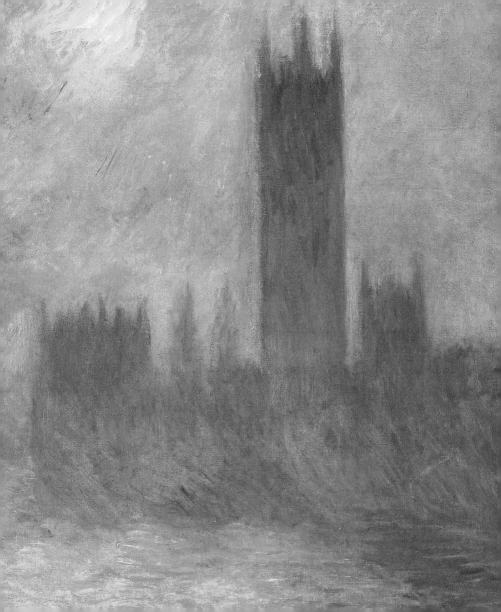

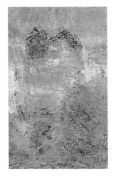

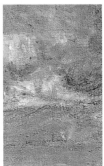

The other part of the cycle was produced in 1893 during a second visit to Rouen, when Monet took with him the canvases he had already executed, intending to add the finishing touches to them. He again studied the movement of light across the portal and, when he saw the effect he wanted, finished the work he had begun a year earlier; where the moment from the past did not recur, he took a fresh canvas and started again from scratch.

The Small Town, Vétheuil

1901
oil on canvas, 90 x 92 cm
The Pushkin Museum of Fine Arts, Moscow

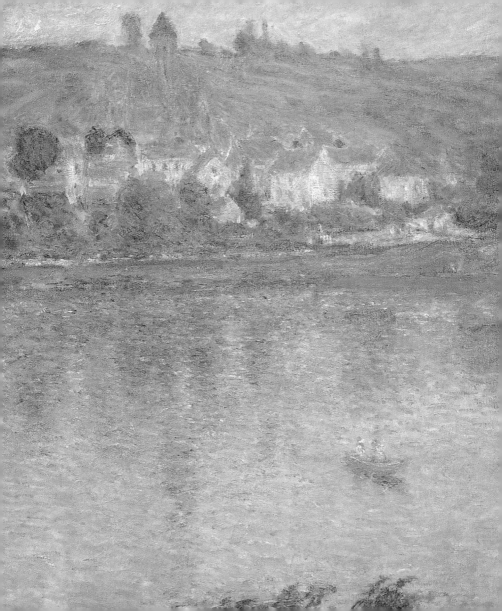

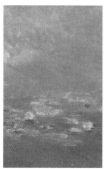

During this second visit Monet did not paint the cathedral only from the viewpoint he had used in 1892; he rented another apartment as well, one which enjoyed a slightly different view of the building.

From here a considerable portion of Saint-Romain's tower was visible to the left of the entrance, and also some houses situated close to the tower.

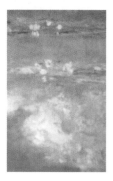

Water-Lilies, Water Landscape, Clouds

1903
oil on canvas, 73 x 100 cm
private collection

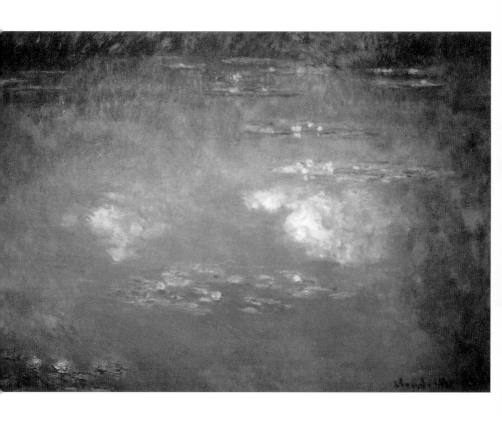

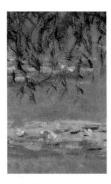

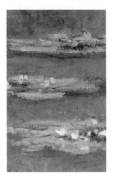

On both his first and second visits Monet turned to his *Cathedrals* with an enthusiasm which bordered on frenzy.

"I am worn out, I can't go on," he wrote to his wife in 1892.

Water-Lilies

―――――――

1903
oil on canvas, 81 x 100 cm
Dayton Art Institute, Dayton, Ohio

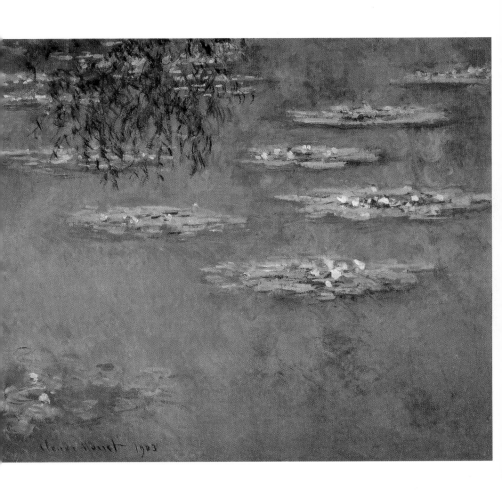

"And, something that I have never experienced before, I have spent a night filled with nightmarish dreams: the cathedral kept falling on me, and at times it seemed blue, at others pink, at others yellow."

Waterloo Bridge, Effect of Fog

1903
oil on canvas, 65 x 100 cm
The Hermitage, Saint Petersburg

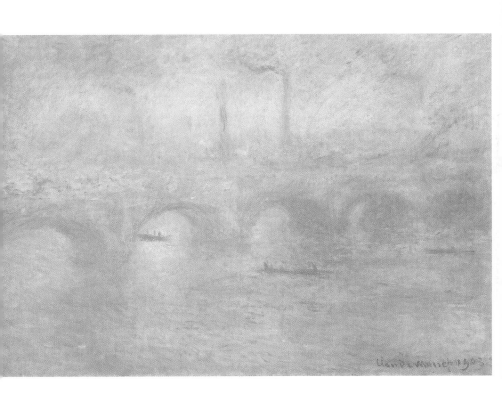

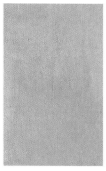

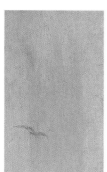

Over the years, work in the studio became increasingly important for the artist. It is unlikely that the canvases executed in Rouen in 1892 remained untouched in Giverny, and it is certain that after his return from the second visit to Rouen he was still bringing them to perfection.

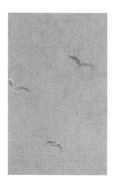

Sea-Gulls
(The Thames in London. The Houses of Parliament)

1904
oil on canvas, 82 x 92 cm
The Pushkin Museum of Fine Arts, Moscow

In 1894, he considered the cycle finished. While on the Riviera in 1888 Monet wrote to Rodin: "I am arming myself and doing battle with the sun... Here one ought to paint with pure gold and precious stones."

London, the Houses of Parliament
Effects of Sunlight in Fog
_____

1904
oil on canvas, 81 x 92 cm
Musée d'Orsay, Paris

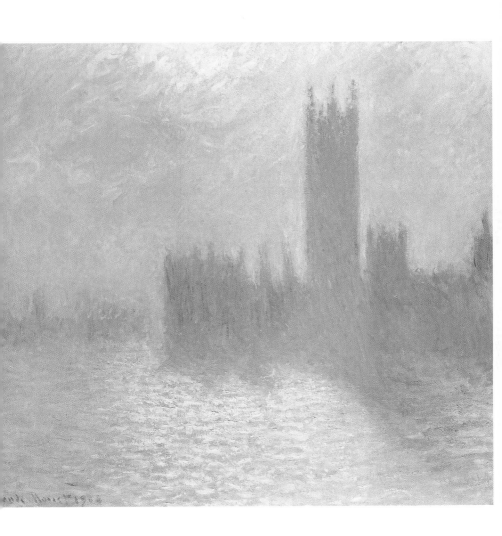

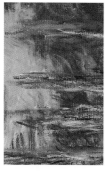

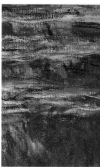

These words could be related to the *Rouen Cathedral* series as well, for here too Monet was waging war with the sun, and the surfaces of the canvases really are reminiscent of a scattering of precious stones being played upon by rays of sunlight.

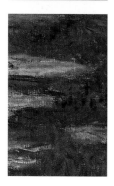

Water-Lilies

1907
oil on canvas, 100 x 73 cm
Bridgestone Museum of Art
(Ishibashi Foundation), Tokyo

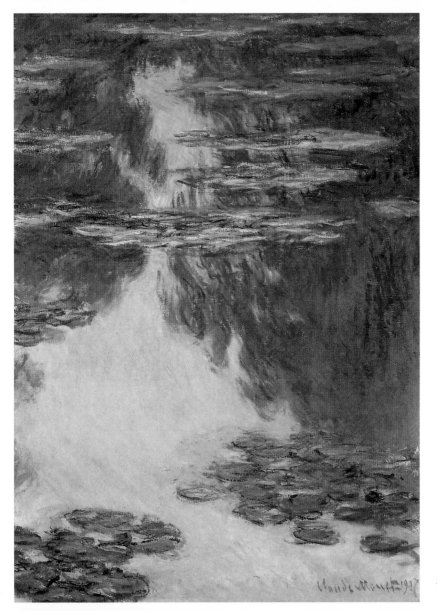

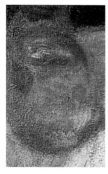

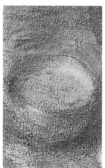

By the time the *Cathedrals* were being created, the nervousness of Monet's brushstrokes and the intensity of his colour combinations had lessened noticeably, and he was now more concerned with shades and nuances of colour.

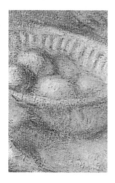

The Eggs
─────────
1907
oil on canvas, 73 x 92 cm
private collection, USA

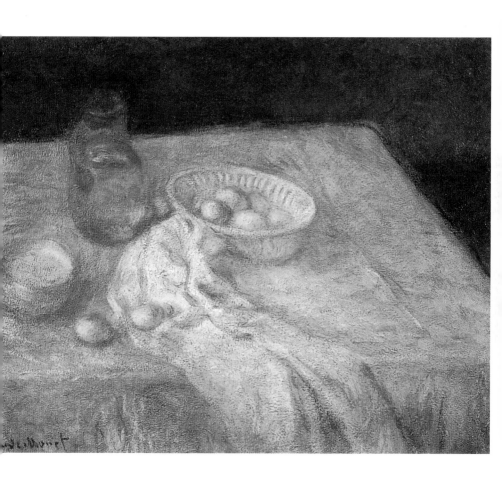

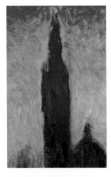

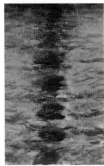

O. Reuterswärd has perceptively noted that one of the most remarkable features of the series lies in the variations of values: "…spots of paint, both strong and weak in terms of light, interlacing in ever-new combinations of tones, the vivid play of colours conveying almost imperceptible light effects."

San Giorgio Maggiore at Dusk

1908
oil on canvas, 65 x 92 cm
National Museum of Wales, Cardiff

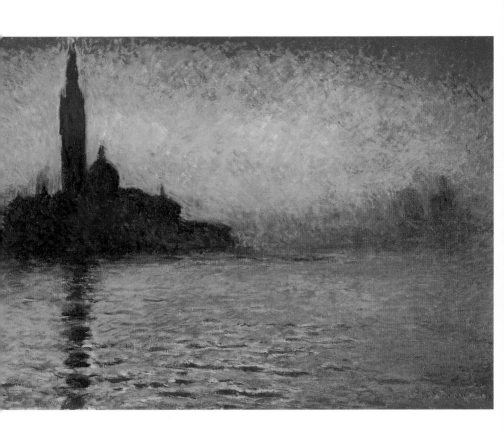

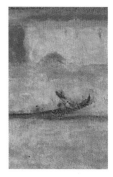

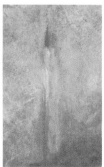

The following years saw no fundamental changes in Monet's career, though the artist continued to experiment in spite of his age. As before, the central role in his art was played by series which he displayed to the public periodically: in 1904 showing views of the Thames at Durand-Ruel's; in 1909 the cycle of *Water-Lilies* at the same venue; and in 1912 views of Venice at Bernheim-Jeune's.

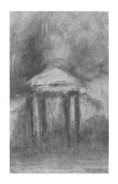

San Giorgio Maggiore

1908
oil on canvas, 60 x 80 cm
National Museum of Wales, Cardiff

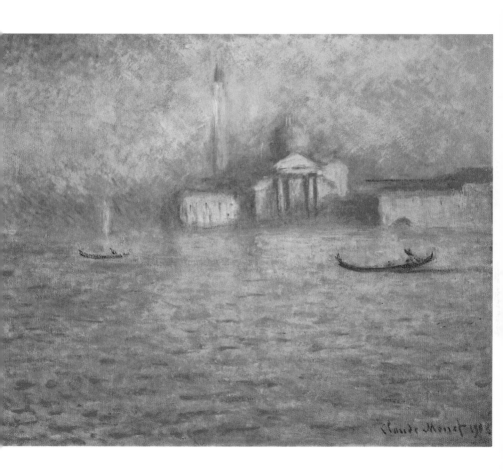

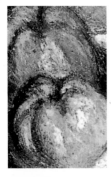

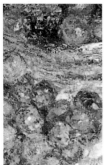

Monet's now increasing, now diminishing colour modulations attune the viewer to a particularly musical wavelength and create a sort of "melody in colour". Perhaps the most notable of all Monet's later series is his *Water-Lilies*, if only because he laboured over it for several decades right up until his death. Monet conceived the idea of the series in 1890.

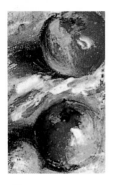

Still Life: Apples and Grapes

1879
oil on canvas, 65 x 81.5 cm
The Art Institute of Chicago, Chicago

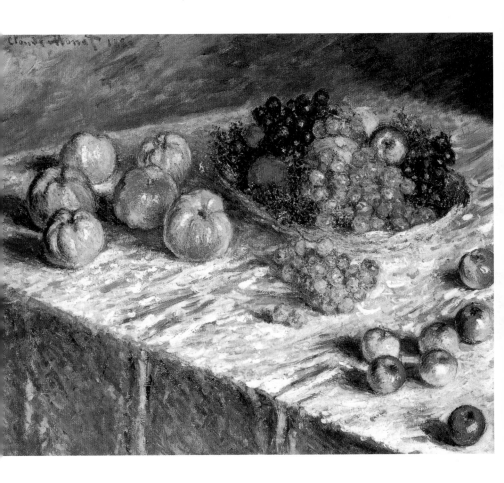

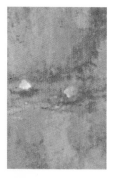

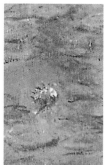

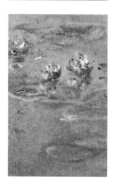

Work on the *Water-Lilies* proper took place in two stages. The first cycle includes canvases of comparatively small dimensions executed between 1898 and 1908; the second stage coincided with the later years of Monet's life, from 1916 to 1926, and includes the huge canvases presented by the artist to the French state in 1922 which now hang in the Orangerie des Tuileries in Paris.

Water-Lilies
────────────

1908
oil on canvas, 92 x 90 cm
Worcester Art Museum, Worcester
Massachusetts

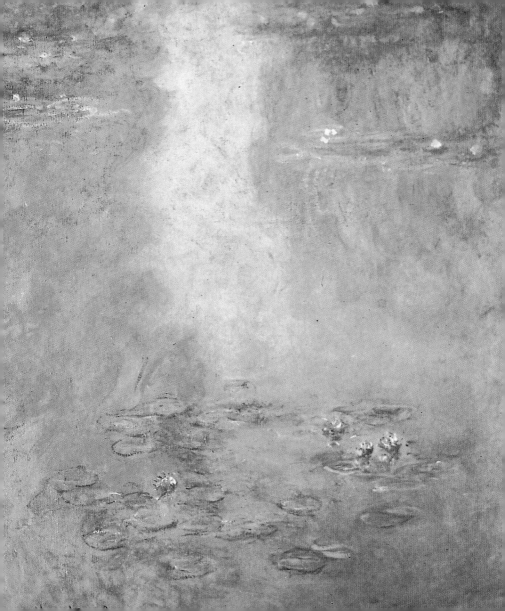

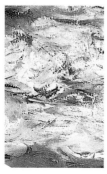

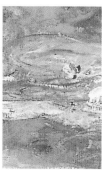

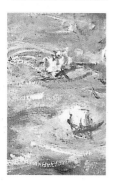

Monet's interest in the motif of water-lilies is most revealing in terms of his mature period.

The images of wild crags and expanses of sea that had previously captivated him had already disappeared from his art, and the meadows of the Ile-de-France with their waving grass and the busy stretches of the Seine were also by now rarely encountered.

Water-Lilies

1908
oil on canvas, diameter (tondo) 81 cm
Dallas Museum of Arts, Dallas

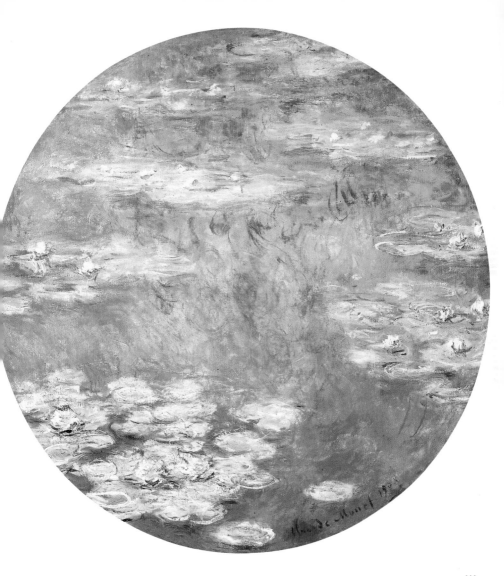

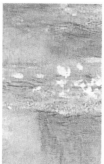

Instead he liked to paint misty London, or Venice reflected in the waters of the lagoon. But above all he was drawn to the bright and beautiful face of his own garden at Giverny. (The author of these lines has been fortunate enough to visit the garden which, now separated from Monet's house by a fence, even today makes a strong impression.

Water-Lilies

1908
oil on canvas, 90 x 92 cm
private collection, Japan

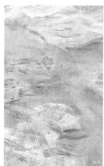

One can imagine how luxuriant it must have looked in Monet's time when the artist, his family and several gardeners looked after it!). Henceforth it was in this refined and fragrant world that the aged Monet was to seek inspiration.

Water-Lilies

1908
oil on canvas, 92 x 90 cm
Worcester Art Museum, Worcester
Massachusetts

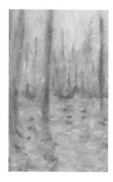

He nonetheless remained an Impressionist. In contrast to the Fauvists he did not turn to the use of spots of colour; his tints remained pure, albeit modulated, for he continued to convey colours by means of abrupt, typically Impressionist brushstrokes.

The Grand Canal

1908
oil on canvas, 73 x 92 cm
Museum of Fine Arts, Boston
Massachusetts

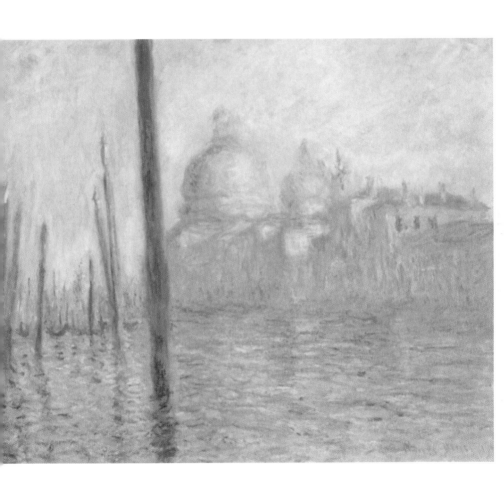

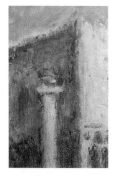

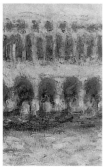

Monet's long life made him a contemporary of all the artistic manifestations of the late nineteenth and early twentieth centuries. Many of the Post-Impressionists rated Monet highly, felt his influence, and even wanted, like Paul Signac and Louis Anquetin, to become his pupils.

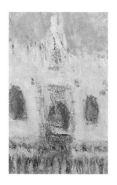

The Doge's Palace

1908
oil on canvas, 73 x 92 cm
private collection of Mr and
Mrs Herbert J. Klapper, USA

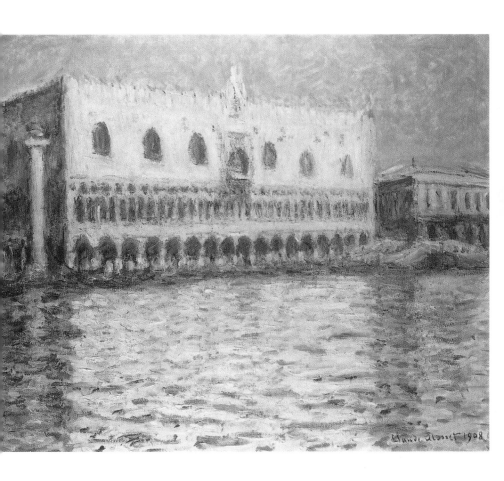

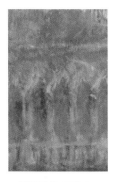

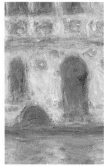

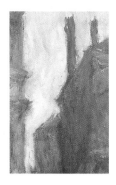

Monet, however, avoided all opportunities to give recommendations or advice. Indeed, the words spoken to a journalist from *Excelsior* in 1920 reflect an attitude to the teaching of painting maintained by him over the course of his whole career:

The Dario Palace

1908
oil on canvas, 65 x 81 cm
The Art Institute of Chicago

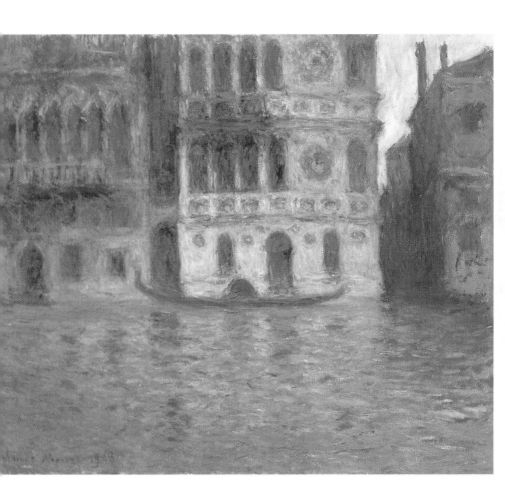

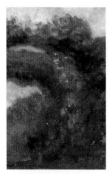

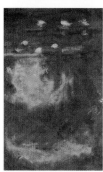

"Advise them to paint as they can and as much as they can without being afraid of poor results... If their painting does not improve of its own accord, then nothing can be done... and I could alter nothing."

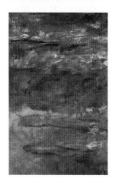

The Blooming Arches, Giverny

1913
oil on canvas, 81 x 92 cm
Phoenix Art Museum, Phoenix, Arizona

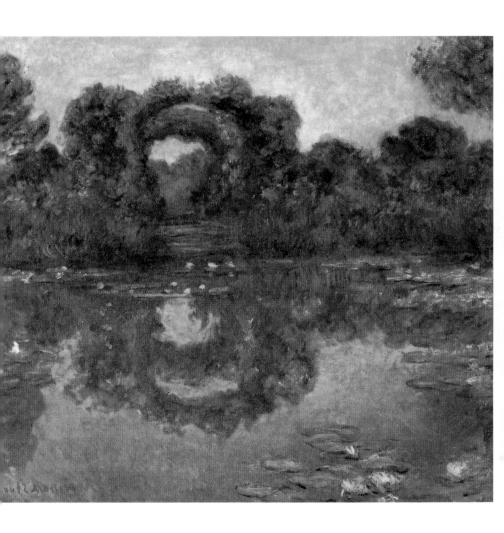

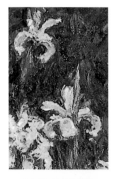

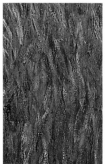

He then added: "The techniques change, but art remains the same: it is the free and emotional interpretation of Nature."

Impressionism, as one of the most vivid manifestations of nineteenth-century Realism, undeniably belongs to this category, and the art of Monet was at the core of the whole Impressionist movement.

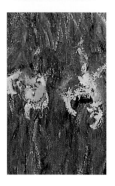

Yellow Irises
_____

1914-1917
oil on canvas, 200 x 100 cm
National Museum of Western Art, Tokyo

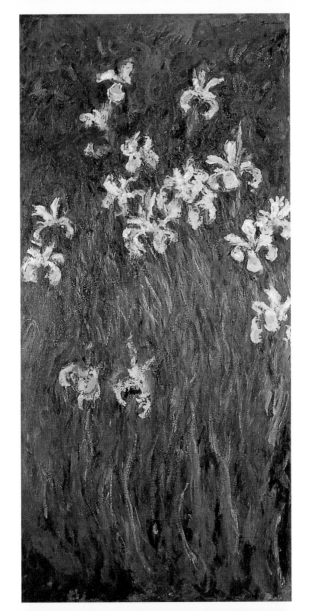

Index

U